W9-BSX-688

THE STORY OF
FESTER CAT

This Large Print Book carries the
Seal of Approval of N.A.V.H.

THE STORY OF FESTER CAT

PAUL MAGRS

THORNDIKE PRESS

A part of Gale, Cengage Learning

GALE
CENGAGE Learning·

Farmington Hills, Mich • San Francisco • New York • Waterville, Maine
Meriden, Conn • Mason, Ohio • Chicago

GALE
CENGAGE Learning®

LIBRARY OF CONGRESS CATALOGING-IN-PUBLICATION DATA

Magrs, Paul, 1969–
  The story of Fester cat / by Paul Magrs.
    pages cm — (Thorndike press large print nonfiction)
  "Thorndike Press® Large Print Nonfiction."
  ISBN 978-1-4104-7833-7 (hardcover) — ISBN 1-4104-7833-5 (hardcover)
  1. Cats—Anecdotes. 2. Human-animal relationships—Anecdotes. 3. Cat owners—Anecdotes. I. Title.
SF445.5.M335 2015
636.8—dc23   2015001664

Published in 2015 by arrangement with The Berkley Publishing Group, an imprint of Penguin Publishing Group, a division of Penguin Random House LLC

Printed in Mexico
1 2 3 4 5 6 7 19 18 17 16 15

THE STORY OF
FESTER CAT

Ungow!

I read a cat book a couple of years ago. Paul asked me to review one or two on his blog for him. He was like, "Look, Fester, you spend all that time lying on my chest when I'm reading. When I'm on the bed settee in the Beach House at the bottom of our garden, I'm reading and you're lying on me. I've got to hold the book up over your head because you're lying there, as close as you can get, until our noses are touching just about, and your paws are right under your chin."

"Yeah, so what?" I said.

And he goes, "Well, while you're lying about, maybe you could read some of these cat books for me. Maybe review them on my blog? It would be good to get a proper cat's point of view."

Well, I am a proper cat. That's very true. I'm a cat!

And I've been one for quite a long time, as it turns out. Last time I went to see Mr. Joe the hairdresser I had a peek at my notes and they were saying there that I was probably about eighteen. Eighteen! What's that? About a hundred and fifty in human years? Probably. But I'm not one of them who goes on as if they're old, if you know what I mean? I'm nimble and trim and I can still run about at a fair clip. So, you know, people never really know my age.

Anyhow, I know Mr. Joe's not really the hairdresser. I know he's a vet. In a little shop on the Stockport Road. These two I live with — this daft pair — they hark on that I'm going to the hairdresser's when they have to take me for pills or to give blood or have a checkup, whatever. I don't know how

8

the hairdresser thing started. Oh, maybe because he shaves a patch of fur under my chin to take blood (right in my Special Spot, as it happens, just as if Mr. Joe knows it's the most delicious spot to have tickled).

So, Paul was like, "Review some cat books why don't you, Fester?" And then he suggested this one about a cat who got on buses. He waited in the queue outside his owner's house every day, apparently. And then jumped aboard the bus and went all over the city and people got to know him. Sounded pretty daft to me. You'd never catch me doing that. And then at the end some awful taxi driver runs the poor devil over and that's the end of that. Well, I blame the owner, really. She had a houseful of cats and didn't look after her commuting cat enough. I mean, I hear that the buses and some people round here can be pretty rough. No way would Paul and Jeremy let me get on those unsupervised. And I wouldn't want to.

I don't think this book about the bus cat was set in Manchester, though. I reckon it was pretty far away from here. Some dump down south where I've never been.

And this is the important part — this old wife who wrote the book — she was all pretty mawkish and stuff because her cat was dead and everything. She was full of regrets like, "Oh, why did I let him get on public transport unsupervised every day!" etc.

But then, in her book, she has these bits where the bloomin' cat writes his own chapters! He writes letters from some kind of heaven . . . !

I mean, what's that about?

He was on about sitting on the rainbow bridge and sending these letters back to his beloved owner and all her friends and — oh yeah — the readers of her bloomin' awful book.

Rainbow bridge, my bum.

I thought back then, when I was reading that book and reviewing it for Paul's blog, it won't be like that. No decent cat would think very much of a rainbow bridge. I certainly wouldn't walk on such a thing. Garish and not very solid.

Down the middle of our garden we've got a plank. I dunno where it came from. Jeremy's always got bits and pieces of DIY and gardening stuff lying about, which is great. Anyway, for as long as we can all remember, this plank has been Fester's plank. Nowadays it's laid across the lawn diagonally between the shaded walk from the terrace, beside the pond wall, and it goes all the way to the Beach House. It's a long, slightly muddy, sun-faded piece of wood that is great for scratching your claws and stretching out your body on.

And what I do is, I sit right in the middle of it. When the sun is full upon it I lie there and soak up all the light and heat and sometimes I doze, but what I do mostly is sit there and from my spot on that plank I can see the whole garden. I can see Paul working or reading in the Beach House or I can look back at the terrace where Jeremy might be reading the paper at the patio table, or diddling about with shovels and plants. He likes to move plants around and wear old clothes that he gets really filthy. He digs up all sorts of interesting stuff.

Also from there I can see the back of the house and the open windows and doors. The kitchen door is open at the top of the back stairs and any moment I like I can trot back down the garden and have a snack at Fester's feeding station. These two fellas make up gags about Fester's running buffet, but we all know it's important I have food there all the time, just whenever I want it. It's Fester's smorgasbord. But I've got a thyroid problem, right? That's what all the hairdresser stuff is about.

I can see the pond and maybe those frogs

gadding about. I've got easy access to Poo Corner, should the mood take me. And I look up into the branches of the magnolia and the larch. Watching for those squirrels and what they get up to. I've a complicated relationship with the squirrels running rampant all over the trees of where we live in Levenshulme, but on the whole I guess they're all right. They're just getting by, I suppose. These are tough days for everyone, I've heard people say. The squirrels have to get along and survive, same as everyone else. So I've given up trying to catch them.

So the point is — my plank. I'm a materialist, I'm a realist. I don't believe in rainbow bridges and cats sitting up there in cat heaven writing letters home after they're dead. I don't believe they write to their owners and say, "Blessings from the celestial beyond from your moggy who still loves you, even if you did let him get run over by a bloomin' cabdriver."

I think, if it's like anything, it'll be like sitting here, on my plank, with the whole world spread out around me. From here I can see nearly all of my world, and I'm happy because the sun's out a bit today — it's the start of spring. It'll be my eighth summer here in this house with these two. And from here I can watch them doing the things they like to do.

And if it ever comes to it and I have to die, if my life turns into anything at all, I'd be happy enough if it was just this. Me being in the garden forever, with this daft pair, like this.

Oh, with the sound of that seventies radio station drifting out from the kitchen. They've got that on all the bloomin' time. I guess I've been brainwashed and now I love all those silly songs as much as they do. At some point I'll tell you about Cat Discos at Lunchtime.

I'll tell you the whole lot. I might as well, mightn't I? Doing those scathing reviews of other people's cat books on Paul's blog has given me the taste for expressing myself. Writing's pretty easy, I reckon, whatever that dafty says.

So I'll tell you everything I can remember about our lives here together.

Ungow!!

MYSTERY

Although I'm not like the cats in those books, today I feel like there's a mystery going on. I've got all the clues like a cat detective. I'm like in one of those American novels where the cat is the cleverest character of them all and he pieces it all together and reveals the solution at the very end.

But my head is banging today. I've had a headache for days and I can't shift it. My eyesight's not right, either. There's quite a few things been going wrong this week. It's not been one of my favourite weeks, I must say.

And the worst thing about that is that the sun's been coming out. Weird weather, this year. Last weekend we even had snow. We so rarely get snow in south Manchester. I don't know why. When it falls it feels like a novelty. By the time it rolls around each year I've forgotten what it is. And I'm like — hey! What's that? — all over again.

Monday it snowed almost horizontal. A very quiet blizzard through the morning. We were indoors, in the front room. Paul was trying to write downstairs because Jeremy had started — actually started! — doing DIY in the little room at the front of the house. Pictures were down, paintbrushes were out, and Paul was downstairs with his laptop, doing his work. I sat on his lap between him and the laptop and then I sat beside him on a blanky for a while. Then I got up and had a snack and I walked back into the front room and he was still going, but the snow had stopped. I could see through the big front window that the snow was petering out and the sun was coming through the trees at last. It was streaming over the houses and the trees at the bottom of our garden and it was slanting into the room. Golden, luscious, warming sunlight. So I charged over there and hopped onto the back of the armchair so I could stretch out in that light.

Paul joined me there. He put his chin on the back of the chair and his arm around me. I let him. I didn't squirm away. I let him ruffle my fur up. And we just sat there for a while. Until the next load of clouds came over. He said something about the weather changing at last and how it should be spring by now. He said the snowdrops in the window boxes and planters had withered, but the anemones were holding up, even in the snow. Yeah, yeah, I thought. You don't even know about gardening. Jeremy planted bulbs in those boxes and you just thought those things had grown there spontaneously. But I snuggled in. I had that headache coming on and the hug was good.

It was a headache like I get in the middle of the night. When my mouth is parched and I know I have to make the trip up the length of the bed, up to Paul's pillows and then hop over to his bedside table. I can perch there, with my whole body curled up and my head in his water glass. He often wakes at the sound of my lapping. Sometimes I have to be extra loud because the water level's gone down and I need him to top it up. He keeps a bottle of spare water on hand. I think it's what he drinks from when he gets thirsty. For some reason he's gone off drinking out of his glass.

One night just before last weekend — I sat there on that bedside table, having had my drink. I just sat there in the middle of the night and I didn't have a clue what I was doing there, or where I should go next. I remember looking from the water glass to the bookcase on Paul's side, and his wardrobe, and Jeremy's messy wardrobe and all the bookcases at the bottom of the bed, and then the bed itself with the tangled blankets and the two of them underneath. They were both awake by then and looking at me. Paul clicked his light on and they both looked concerned. I guess I was moving my head from side to side and casting about like I didn't know what I was doing.

"What's up, Fester Cat?"

Then I was reminded that I had to go and lie on Paul's knees and then in the crook of his legs and fall asleep until first light. It all came back to me and I was suddenly relieved. Ungow! I hopped back over and that was okay. It was fine. But it was a scary moment and the headache stayed with me when I woke up. It went away a little but it kept coming back and I knew it had to do with that raging thirst that keeps coming over me.

Monday morning and we're sitting in the sun until the snow clouds cover it, and Paul decides we should take a walk down the garden. It feels daring after all the cold and snow. Some parts of the country have been snowbound all weekend. But when we crack open the back door and look out — the patio is dry. It's not right hot or anything, but it's dry and oh, the smell of the garden is wonderful. I can feel my nose doing that dimpling thing and I'm breathing faster as I sit there on the back doorstep. I love it and it always makes Paul laugh. He says I'm sniffing the news from outside. I guess that's right. You can tell a lot of what's been going on from the smells outside.

Down the garden we go. Down the crazy paving path Jeremy built, between the little walls he made out of old red bricks and the urns of herbs — all a bit frosty and dead by now. There's a skin of ice on the pond and I reckon all last year's frogs will be dead. Or do they sleep underwater? I don't even know.

Down the plank. Look at the magnolia, and the buds are there but nowhere near out yet. They're curled up tight on the knuckly, dark branches. Paul is opening the Beach House door, dragging it open, and it takes some doing. The wood has swollen in the cold and wet.

The cool air and warm sun are making my headache lift away. I hop onto the veranda of the little house and then I can smell last summer's scents coming out of there. It's all damp books and trapped sun and dust and cat hair, mellow wood and dry soil. It's wonderful — and here comes

18

the sun again, sliding through the dusty panes.

Paul sits on the bed settee, trying to write with his laptop. I jump on my wickerwork chair and my cushion smells divine. After a while of gentle dozing, I jump over to sit in the crook of his legs. Hey, I nudge him and my nose feels dry. This is the first day of spring, probably. This is the first afternoon we get to spend out here. The first of many, all over again. It'll be our eighth summer here together.

He's distracted, though. Off in that world of his own. He's sitting up awkwardly, typing with one hand and giving himself backache and neck ache. But he never moves his legs and so I don't have to move.

That was the Monday things started to seem funny. Last Monday. I wobbled a bit, swaying, as we went back down the garden, only an hour later. I dithered a bit on the patio. I know I did, and I know Paul noticed.

I sat on the back stairs and I had this amazing thought. I think the sun brought it to me as the clouds cleared once more.

It was: I've not had a tummy tickle in so long. What's that about? I love them! I crave them. I always have. And yet I can't remember the last time I flung myself onto the ground in an almighty flomp and shouted

19

at that pair to come and tickle me daft.

I guess I've been feeling a bit less cushioned. I lost weight before Christmas and then again recently. I feel a bit more bony. But how could I forget about all the tickles and rubs? The fur on my stomach was the only bit Paul couldn't get to when he combed out the snags and tangles in my fur recently. I wouldn't lie down. I wouldn't flomp. One night the two of them got down on the front room floor and rolled about on the rug. They were wriggling and shouting "Flomp!" and "Tummy Tickle!" and I just didn't understand. That was last week sometime. I just thought they were being daft, as per usual. But they were actually trying to tell me something and now I remember.

I love flomps! I love flinging myself sideways and landing jaw first and rolling around onto my back with my paws up in the air.

I especially love it on the gritty concrete of the patio or the backdoor steps. There's something immensely satisfying about rubbing the dirt into your fur like humans do shampoo.

Paul is delighted that I've suddenly remembered. He tickles me like crazy and I can't help grinning. I purr so hard I'm almost singing. I arch and wriggle and almost fall sideways off the step. He takes a picture of me on his phone while I'm at my most ticklish and zaps it to Jeremy upstairs.

Then, when I've had enough, I'm like, all right, all right! Don't make a big show of me! Come on. Back inside the kitchen. Food!

My News

It was a busy week as well. There were all sorts of things coming up. It was Jeremy's birthday on Thursday and then it was Easter at the weekend. We didn't have any firm plans but there's always stuff going on round here. I knew that since it was holiday time, the pair wouldn't be going out anywhere. They'd be staying at home and it would be like one great long weekend and they'd be sitting here with me — and so it'd be busy, as far as I was concerned.

But then the Tuesday came and I had to go to the hairdresser's and see Mr. Joe. Well, I've already said that I know he's not really a Mr. Teasy Weasy. I know he's really a vet. I go a bit quiet when I'm there and I stand still on his table, and he's pretty kind. He knows me by now, after almost seven years of being in the care of these two. He dealt with my injections and my thyroid and my teeth and gums when I had to have my operation. So he knows my history and he greets me by name and stuff, which is pretty nice. I give him a quiet "Ungow!," which comes out more like "mow," because I'm feeling dizzy and tired on Tuesday morning.

He tells Jeremy I've had a stroke.

When did that happen?

He says he wants to take a blood test. We should come back tomorrow. No, wait, it's early enough to do it now — it's only ten a.m. We could do the blood now and it'll be back by teatime. Then he can see what's what. He's worried. I can hear it in his tone.

What now? I think.

I've had a couple of infections and bouts of flu in the last couple of years. My first and worst one was about three years ago when they realised my thyroid had gone funny.

So now it's like here's something else and I'm getting my Special Spot under my chin shaved and Mr. Joe is talking to Jeremy and I phase out for a bit. My headache's back, like those clouds rolling over the sun yesterday in the garden. I want some water and I want a wee.

Mild stroke. It was a mild stroke.

But a stroke is something good, isn't it? A stroke is like someone ruffling your fur, or rubbing your ears. This isn't like that. How come they use the same word?

Then we were home and I lay on my pink blanky with my dirtied-up toys and for a while I couldn't be bothered explaining anything or talking to anyone much. I had some fancy cat food for lunch — the stinkiest kind, which was okay. I took my lunchtime tablet in a wodge of pâté and crunched it down without causing a scene.

Then the kitchen ceiling fell in. I was in the front room with Paul and he was kind of patting me and talking to me. Jeremy was upstairs pulling stuff about in the shower room he's making. It's directly above the kitchen, and yeah — it's been ready to go for a while now — all the junk that was held up by plastic sheeting. All this black muck and dust. There was a great big crash and it all came down.

Me and Paul thought the sky was falling in.

The worst of the mess was in the kitchen, of course. But even in the front room we were like sneezing all afternoon, the two of us.

Paul tried to do some cleaning. I guess he was a bit manic, cleaning the surfaces and stuff. I guess he was making the time go faster until my next appointment at 5:50, when we had to go back for the blood results.

When it came to being back at the vet's, it was all very serious. Mr. Joe and Jeremy were talking away and I didn't really follow much of it. All I remember is Jeremy getting these, like, free cat-food pouches from the lady at the counter when we were leaving. I was in my Selfridges travel case, but I could still see out enough to clock that there was cat-food buying going on. It was like gourmet stuff in silver pouches that I knew I'd never tried before.

Not bad, I thought!

We went home and I heard Paul asking stuff and Jeremy saying, in that very calm way of his, "Let me get him out before I explain." And he opened the box and out I sprang onto the pine table, which Paul had cleaned of all that black dust and gunk. Ta-da! Here I am! Ungow! It's way beyond teatime! Where's this new gourmet stuff?

And it was all right, actually. Didn't taste too bad at all. Could have done with a bit more seasoning, I thought. And it was a lot sloppier than Whiskas. Jeremy said that was the point. No salt. I'm not allowed any salt.

The two of them were talking seriously now. I just had my bit of tea and slipped into the front room. I don't like it when they

25

talk like that, like they're keeping stuff from me. I'm buggered if I'm sitting around listening for snippets. Best clearing off altogether until they decide to tell me properly what's up.

The headache came back and I went away to the cupboard in Paul's little study. I went into the corner until my head cleared. By then it was like the middle of the night.

I popped into the bathroom and saw they'd put down new rugs. The little tray was waiting there but I couldn't be doing with that. I did a poo on one rug and a long wee on the white rug from Habitat. Gave them both a bit of a sniff. Okay. Bedtime proper, now.

I went into the boys' room and they were both fast asleep.

Jeremy snores like an elephant snorting a bathful of jelly up its trunk. But I guess I'm used to how noisy humans can be. He's also kind of restless in the night, jumping about and changing position.

That's why, for six years or more, I have slept on the blue blanky on Paul's side of the bed. He hardly moves at all in his sleep and he sleeps with his legs conveniently folded to one side. I've taught him to do that! So on nights like this, when I come to sleep beside him — I can take a swift drink at his water glass and then hop onto the bed. And I know he'll have already made a space for me. Halfway down the bed, facing the window, wide enough for me to lie sideways.

Ungow! He woke up and looked so pleased to see me. Go back to sleep, I tell him. And I purr at him, going "sing sing" until he does.

This is a busy week. We've a birthday in the household and a special diet to start and people visiting, I think, and a long weekend. We all need our sleep. We all need a good rest.

This is the stillest, most perfect night, though. It's three o'clock in the morning and it's just about a full moon tonight, so there's light on Fester's garden. From here on the bed I can see the houses out back, the swaying trees, and the roof of the Beach House.

Paul goes back to sleep — and I start to follow him. I carry on purring. It's like I'm telling a story to myself. That's how I sound when I'm doing singing like this.

And I reckon I've got a story to tell.

Tonight is when I'll tell it.

MY FAVOURITE THINGS

Things start happening pretty quickly after that, even though I personally get slower.

Wednesday's not a great day, though thinking back, I got to do all my favourite, usual things, only a bit more carefully and gradually. I ate a whole pouch of that new cat food. It was beefy flavour and there was some fuss because I wanted more than just one pouch and it turns out Mr. Joe had stipulated only one pouch a day.

I was shouting, "Mow! Mow! Ungow!"

I stood there incredulously at my feeding station, staring at my empty smorgasboard. What was this? What else was I going to eat?

Paul was manically cleaning kitchen surfaces and then cooking human food. Choosing something I just wouldn't be interested in, on purpose, I reckon. Then we gathered together in the front room and we watched *Frasier*. They're up to Season Seven again and Daphne's wedding. I sat on their knees one at a time. Yeah, looking back, Wednesday wasn't so bad.

My two back legs were wonky, though. When I went upstairs to do a poo and a wee on the rugs, my legs were kind of out of sync. I wasn't happy on the stairs. Also — aaarrgghh — my claws were too long. Last time at the hairdresser's Mr. Joe was good enough to give them an expert, professional, no-nonsense clipping. And afterwards I wasn't snagging myself on carpets, blankies, table mats. But he didn't do them during my visit this week and I was a bit like, huh? But claw clipping is what really needs doing. It's all very well giving out new diets and shaving patches of fur — but what about all this snagging and snarling? I just about twisted my front legs off coming down the stairs.

Actually, I was happier when Paul carried me up the stairs and down again. I feel woozier than I did yesterday.

Also, he fetched out their human nail clippers and tried to get me to cooperate. I did after a while, but he was a bit tentative and it annoyed me. Then he was grimacing and flinching because of the noise when you clip cat claws. They make a grisly crunching noise. At least he was careful to avoid the black bits. These are blood vessels and mustn't be cut into. When I last had them done by Mr. Joe, he made a comment on the very fine, visible blood vessels in my claws, as I recall.

Anyhow, Paul did his best and managed to trim my front two paws.

By nighttime I was exhausted. I just went under the cupboard in Paul's study to sleep.

He fetched me out at six in the morning, at first light. He thought I'd want to hear the birdsong in the back garden and to smell the fresh air coming in. The window was wide open, because apparently Jeremy snores less if the window's open. What's that about? But I loved the sounds of Fester's garden and I snoozed on Paul.

When I woke up properly for Thursday things felt different. I did a lot of purring to make the boys feel okay about it.

When they asked and petted me and carried me about and stuff, I made sure they knew I was still singing. But I felt awful. The headache and my eyes spinning. And the stairs were out of the question. My back legs were crazy. Three steps at a time even on a level landing were quite enough.

In the bathroom I did a poo, but at first I couldn't move away from it. I felt humiliated. Paul was with me and he carried me away, cuddling me. I was pretty proud of that poo on the new diet — because I'd been quite bunged up before that. Widdling is a problem, though. I'm doing really little widdles, which is weird. Paul and Jeremy take turns having a wee in their toilet to encourage me. They say I can pick any rug I want and piss on it to my heart's content. They're pretty daft.

But the important thing about Thursday really was that it was Jeremy's birthday. Ungow! He's forty-six now, which, I gather, in human years is pretty ancient. I lay on the bed at sevenish, and Panda was there, too, going on like he does: "Many felicitations on your birthday, Jeremy. Here are presents that Paul and I and the cat have chosen and bought for you, plus a card that Paul has made, which isn't as good as last year's, which featured a picture of me on it." (I'll explain about Panda later.)

Jeremy opened his presents and they had a cup of tea. One of his presents was a silly fluffy toy that looked a bit like a black-and-white cat. Though Panda said it was more like a penguin with pointy ears. I shuffled over and let Jeremy do a bit of cat Reiki on my face and I nudged his hand and his face and I gave his nose a lick. Why do I have this compulsion to clean Jeremy's nose? Even I don't know. It just comes over me.

We were all together on the bed. With the sun coming through.

Later in the day, people came round. Jamie and Kyle came and they had a look at me and by then I was tired, on my settee on my pink blanket. They had a look and patted me and heard about how my walking and stuff had gone a bit wobbly. And how I was building myself up with new pills and a new diet.

They were out to lunch at some deli place round the corner. I heard they had spicy cider and chocolate cake. They came back pretty soon, but I was okay. I watched them eating chocolates and having tea in the front room.

Then there were others — Karen from down our street, who pops in when the boys are away. And Jeremy's pal Penny. We were all in the kitchen and the table had all these birthday cards on it, and wrapping paper and Easter eggs people had brought. Jeremy lifted me up onto the table and I could see everyone then. I could look them in the eye and hear what they were saying. Ungow! I always like to know what's going on.

I walked up and down that table, like I always do, weaving between the obstacles. There's always loads of crap lying around in our house. Don't get me wrong, it's always interesting crap. Messy, but wonderful. I love it here. I've always loved living in our house with all this stuff.

I weaved and wobbled down the table and shouted "Ungow!" at all our visitors. It's just something I have to do. If someone comes visiting, then it's only polite, isn't it? Saying hello and seeing how they are. I like to keep sociable, and even though I was feeling so rough by then, I made sure I kept my standards up.

When we were all alone — just Jeremy and Paul and Panda and me and it was the evening — I relaxed. I was exhausted. All I wanted to do was get under that cupboard in all the cat hairs and dust and sleep as long as I could. Mortified they had to help me in the bathroom. I tried to remember about the litter tray. I made a big effort to hop into it, but nothing was doing. I kind of fell sideways onto the rug.

HEROES

Friday was all about sitting downstairs. It was Good Friday. A human holiday. No one was working today. (Apart from those awful men fixing up a rooftop at the back of the house. They were banging away and using a drill. Which can be pretty annoying when your head is banging like mine.)

I lay in Paul's lap in the sunny living room. All my legs were funny now. He had to tuck them in under me, helping me to sit nicely on his lap. I cuddled in and purred as loudly and as fiercely as I could manage.

Paul sat very nicely. He put on movie after movie that day. We watched *The Never-Ending Story, Time Bandits,* and *Willow.* It was all kids' stuff. Sometimes weepy, sometimes exciting, nice and loud and silly and always interesting. I dozed sometimes and then I was awake and getting back on with telling my story and sing-singing as hard as I could.

I'd gone off those gourmet pouches from the hairdresser's. Today's was supposed to be chicken flavour, but I didn't like it much at all. Mr. Joe had said only 50 percent of cats can stomach these silver pouches. I'd had two days trying them out. I could tell the boys were disappointed, but really. I wasn't into them at all.

Jeremy went out in the car.

Did I ever tell you that when he goes to the nearest supermarket in the car, picking up ciggies, the paper, sweets and treats and top-up groceries — did I tell you that he calls it El Shoppo? I've absolutely no idea why. It's not even like a Mexican place or anything. It's just one of those things he does.

While he was out, Paul sat with me and he was talking about all this stuff. I realised quite quickly that he was talking about when I first moved in here with them. When I decided to adopt the pair of them. He was going into all the details and telling me everything about myself and our times together. I was a bit like, Ungow! I know all this! If you'd have stayed awake the other night you'd have heard me singing about it all! When the full moon was out and I lay on the bed.

But he kept on talking and he started

laughing and crying at different parts. He looked at my eyes and I guess they were doing that flicky thing still. My head was pounding, but I went on listening. There was some stuff he said I think I'd forgotten. Thing is, when you're a cat, you can't really write stuff down to remind you. You can scratch things, you can spray them, piss on them, or bum them up. And every little thing you do tells a story. But Paul has this mania for detail and writing every little thing down. So while Jeremy was out at El Shoppo he just talked and talked up a storm and it was all about me. Ungow!

Well, soon enough Jeremy came back with a huge load of orange carrier bags. They were stuffed full. He brought chicken roll and sliced ham and pâté. He brought tuna and corned beef and smoked salmon. He brought me trout. Fresh, wonderful, pale orange, fragrant trout!

It's my favourite food in the whole world! Ungow!

I wolfed it up. I almost had his fingers off, whoever gave it to me.

It was big flakes of trout.

Actually, it wasn't all that much I ate. Maybe a few mouthfuls.

It was the sweetest, rarest food I ever tasted in my life.

And after that I stayed put and I dozed on the big settee. And Paul lay down with me and he dozed as well, holding me tucked against his body.

The evening ran by, as evenings do. Jeremy went out to one of his meetings about saving Levenshulme Baths and Library. It's been a big project this winter and he's been out at lots of meetings. It's got him out of the house, which Paul and I have been pleased about. He was getting stuck in a rut, and since he started with this campaign marvelous things have happened. His confidence has come back to him, after two rough years. The council has adopted his business plan — or something. Something good like that. I didn't quite get all the details, but it was good.

Paul and I watched telly and when we ran out of things we wanted to watch he put on the radio. It's great, it comes on the widescreen telly, so you don't even have to move from your comfy spot. He put on Radio 2 and found that they were doing two hours about his favourite, David Bowie. They had dug out archive recordings of him talking and singing.

All these songs are very familiar to me. I've heard Paul and Jeremy's records many, many times over.

While I was drifting off, David Bowie back in 1977 was saying something about, even though he'd just made a record called *Low* he was very happy in his life as it was. He had escaped all the bad stuff and moved to Berlin. He hoped to carry on being happy, he said. He hoped that his life was going to keep on being as super as it was right now.

And then that song "Heroes" came on.

Sing sing.

THE FARTHEST I'VE BEEN

I went to bed but I didn't want water and I didn't even want a wee. It was all not a bit like me. I didn't feel like purring by then, either. Paul and Jeremy stroked me and stuff but I couldn't make any noises. Not by then.

I lay between them, sinking into the duvet. Almost hidden from them.

I let Paul hold me all night. I moved away, wriggling at one point. I don't know where I think I was going. He came and lay the wrong way up in the bed and held me close and I liked that. In the past I might have found it a bit much, but it was all right.

First light came and I was awake, holding up my head, but it was heavy. It was really pounding something shocking. Jeremy woke up early for a Saturday and lay next to me.

It took quite a lot of energy but I lifted up my paws and put them on his hands. Then I put my chin on my paws. My whole head and paws were in his open hands. Look, I said. Ungow. This is me. This is Fester the Cat. And I'm trusting you guys. I'm putting myself in your hands, just like I did when I moved in and decided I was adopting you two. I'm doing it now when I need to the most.

We lay like that for a long time. Paul went for his bath and made tea.

When he brought it Jeremy went for his bath. It was like our morning routines. It was great. We were getting ready for the day.

Paul picked me up. No, I didn't want the loo.

He carried me downstairs. He opened the back door.

We went out into the garden.

The sun! The sun was coming through the trees and it was brilliant. It was nine o'clock on the day the clocks went forward. It was Saturday and it was the first day of British summertime. And the sun! Look at it on the pond and the Beach House and Fester's plank.

I let Paul carry me out down the garden and we sat in all my favourite places. I even sat on the soil for a while, sniffing up the scent of outdoors, under the magnolia. We sat on my veranda chair and I made a sudden bolt forwards. A surge that almost carried me off his knee. He caught me and set me down where he knew I wanted to be. In the Beach House. He opened the heavy door and my strength couldn't quite get me over the threshold. I sat there gathering it back. But Paul picked me up and took me into that little house that smells of books and old blankets and put me in my bamboo chair. The sun comes through the trellis like diamonds. It's cool hot cool hot cool. I want to lie here forever.

"This will always be Fester's garden," Paul says. He's holding me again. He's carried me back out. He's standing on the lawn, facing the trees, facing the houses out back and the sun coming over the rooftops. We're blinking up the sun, and just drinking it in. It's soaking into my fur. I'm clinging on to his woolly blue cardy. It's new but I've covered it in a decent amount of cat hair. It smells good.

He's saying, "This will always be Fester's garden. It will be where you'll always belong. These past seven summers and us together here, it's like you've made me run away from home, every day. Like I dreamed about doing when I was a boy. Every day you make me run away with a bag of books and pens and my little cat and I hide out in this den, in this little house. And we camp out here all day long. And this is where we'll always be, now. Forever. We belong here and nothing can ever change that. There'll always be a little house at the bottom of a garden in Levenshulme where Fester the Cat dozes and then he gets up to dash about and has a nice sit and says, 'Ungow!' "

Jeremy was on the phone. Talking to a very nice-sounding young lady, he said. He had printed off a not-very-good map from Google Earth. The place we were going was in Cheadle Hulme, near the golf course. Paul said, "It'll be even fancier than your usual hairdresser's, Fester. If it's Cheadle it'll be like some celebrity salon where fancy cats go."

But it meant the car journey was longer. I've never been on such a long car journey. I was in my cat box on Paul's knee and we went much farther than the Stockport Road. In fact, I don't think I've ever been as far as that from home, ever! How strange. See? There's always new stuff to learn and to discover.

We drove down a long road and I was losing my balance a bit inside the box. Jeremy said, "I'll drive as smoothly as I can, Fester Cat!"

And then they sang to me!

First of all Paul was just talking. He kept saying "Ungow! Ungow! Mow mow!" Jeremy told him he was sounding a bit manic. But I didn't mind. My ears twitched up when he started shouting "Ungow." Yes! I thought! Yes! Yes! Ungow! Ungow! I'm here!

"We should sing!" Jeremy said. "Sing, Paul! Sing to him!"

And Paul sang his silly song about Fester Cat being the best cat in the world. They both sang it.

It was like a triumphant song. "Fester Cat! Fester Cat! He's the best cat in the world! Fester Cat!" and they both threw in a few shouted "Ungows!" for good measure.

So, yeah, the map was crap — and the street names weren't printed and the roads were out of proportion. We drove through Cheadle and out towards the railway station, past the golf course. Then on Queen Street we got lost. The very street where the emergency hairdresser's was supposed to be. Jeremy was losing his temper. We nearly ran into another car. There were speed bumps. The car rolled over them bumpily and I wobbled. I almost rolled over completely. Jeremy tried to phone the nice lady again but the sun was glaring on the screen of his phone. He threw his phone onto the backseat, swearing. Paul rang up using his instead.

The nice receptionist said, "Oh, we're not

far after the turn-off into Queen Street."
And they were! Jeremy and Paul looked
around and we were there! We were parked
right outside the emergency vet clinic. "Is it
Fester Cat?" asked the receptionist. Paul
was amazed. "You're getting personal,
luxury service, Fester!"

We parked at the back. Lots of lovely
spaces on a quiet Saturday morning. It was
just after ten.

They carried me in inside my cat box and
Paul was saying about how fancy it was. A
really fancy hairdresser's. I couldn't really
see out of my cat box, which he put on the
counter while Jeremy filled in the forms and
stuff.

Then the lady vet was asking us into her
little office. Off came the roof of my cat box
and I lay there still while they all talked
about me. All this stuff about the week I'd
had. And the nice lady vet said something
about how I must have felt like I'd had the
worst hangover in the world. My head must
be thumping. Yes, yes, I thought! She under-
stands! She knows just how I feel! Ungow!

Paul and Jeremy picked me up, one at a
time. They hugged me. They said all the
things again they've been saying all week.
They told me they loved me. Paul said
much less than he usually does. Now he was

saying, "Thank you, Fester Cat, thank you for everything you've given us. Ungow, Fester."

I lay down again and I was pleased they'd brought the airport blanket that went inside the cat box. It was one from Paul's study. From a corner by the door where I sometimes lie when he's working and I'm waiting for him to stop for lunch or whatever.

So I lay down and they talked some more. And they're both stroking my back and my ears and under my chin. The daft pair. They're going on a bit, actually. We're in a stranger's place and they're acting like we're all at home together. But I don't mind.

There's another woman coming in. A calm girl with the hairdressing clippers and she's doing a patch on my leg. I hear them saying that my headache will clear up pretty quickly after the injection. I'll feel it all fade away and then I can sleep.

Well, that sounds okay to me just now. This bloomin' racket in my head, it's taken away my appetite — my everything — just lately. I lie flat as can be and relax everything. I keep my eyes open, straight ahead. Ungow! I'm staring straight at Paul and Jeremy as they come close and talk and talk and talk.

"Ungow! Fester! Ungow! We love you."

The nice lady vet's telling them that they mustn't be scared if, after I fall asleep, I jump or exhale or do anything strange. And I'm like, What? What am I going to do?

She puts a stethoscope on me — all cool on my ruffled belly, and after a long moment she tells them, "Yes, his heart has stopped." And then she says how she'll leave them with me for as long as they want.

Then I'm with them. I'm with Paul and Jeremy alone in that room we've never visited before. I can't really see them, but my eyes have been funny all week, let's face it. And my headache is gone. It's cleared like the snow clouds and the freezing rain.

And yes — I give out a big sigh, like I often do just at the point of falling asleep. And, a few minutes after my heart and all that other stuff has come to a stop, my rib cage jumps. My whole body flinches.

But that's because I'm running.

Do you know? Do you remember? When you watched me fall asleep on the settee or by the fire or on the plank in the garden? You'd know I was dreaming about running around. I'd pad the air with my paws, my body would jump.

And I'm running right now.

I'm running as fast as I can. I'm running now just because I can.

And I know the way back. Bugger Google Earth. I know the way back north from Cheadle Hulme to Levenshulme. I may not have travelled far in my life. But there's nothing like Cat Nav, is there?

I'm racing back like the clappers up Kingsway, past pizza shops and fried chicken shops. I dash past Burnage and the biscuit factory and the Antiques Village and the Nawaab Curry House. I turn off at Levenshulme station and through the rough streets overrun by cats and I know I'm near home now. I can hear the trains running down the lines towards Piccadilly. The railway lines where I've lived all my life. Ungow! I'm bounding towards the twisty, turning streets where it's all horse chestnut trees and cobbles and red-bricked terraces.

I'm running as fast as I ever ran before and I don't — I won't — stop until Chestnut Avenue.

Paul and Jeremy can catch me up in the car. They know the way.

But I have to get here first, don't I? That's obvious. That's what has to happen now.

And here I am. Bounding down the alleyway. Over cobbles and over fences and shrubs.

Fester's garden is waiting for him.

It's the first day of summer — and that's

official! And I am here. I'm back. I'm back in my place. And I'm going to be here forever now.

Ungow! Ungow!
Ungow!

CATS OF LEVENSHULME

All right, so I was a stray. I hadn't always been one, though. I'd lived in two different households and I'd left both. I'd chosen to leave both. I just got up and left, all right? It was one of those things. I knew I wasn't in the right place. I was like, I'm out of here.

Not that I went all that far. I mean, this is

where I know, right? This is where I belong. I'm a Levenshulme cat. I live in South Manchester. These few leafy streets between the railway lines and Slade Lane — that's the world I belong to. I don't even know what goes on beyond that. But this bit will do me. There are loads of other cats round here, some strays, some who live in homes, some who do a part-time kind of thing. And they all agree. This is the best place you can live round here. So I never saw the point in moving farther afield when I became a stray at the age of twelve, back in 2006.

I stayed put because I knew that I had to. I had a kind of feeling. A premonition.

I did! I truly did. I have always lived my life knowing that something good is gonna turn up. I always knew that the rest of my story was gonna be a good one. I don't know how I knew that, but I always did.

Ungow!

I am Fester the cat. Welcome to my book, everyone!

Bessy the cat — or Aunty Bessy as she liked to be called, her with the big head and the huge massive bollocks, she said, "What makes you think anything good's gonna happen to you? Why should it? Why should anything good happen to any of us?"

She was always pretty gloomy, that Bessy.

She was mixed up and altogether bitter, really. She was a real scrapper. She'd argue with anyone and I used to annoy her back then by being so optimistic.

"Look, your life is terrible! It really sucks! You're homeless like I am. You're scrounging about for this and that. Trying to get by. You've lost all that weight. You've got no teeth. Your gums are rotten and your fur's falling out. And you've got fleas like the rest of us. You're hopping with them and it's worse 'cuz you're allergic and you're like one all-over scab. So what gives you the right to go on like everything's gonna turn out to be all right?"

"Mow . . ." I shrugged. Actually, I was struggling to stay bright and cheery, what with the way Bessy talked. She could be proper mardy. I didn't want to upset her because she was powerful and big and she could give you quite a clout. "I just know everything's gonna be fine: 2006 is my year. I can feel it."

She shook her big head and sighed at me. She pointed out that all the years since 1995 — none of them had been my year, or hers. She'd known me since I was a kitten. She really did belong in my extended family. There's always a lot of black-and-white cats ɔund here in what the humans like to call

Levenshulme's Conservation Area. I like to think we all go back to the original farm cats that must have lived here before most of the houses were built in the late 1800s. We're all the same family — and that's how it feels.

All us classy cats in the black-and-white fur like something out of an old movie from the 1950s. Us kitchen-sink drama cats. We're glossy and pithy and wise as old films.

Bessy can't actually be my aunty, though. Not literally, on account of her having that huge pair of bollocks hanging down. But she certainly carries on like my aunty.

I've joined her little gang. We go around together. We have done all year so far. At the start of 2006 we banded together for some kind of protection. It was a cold, harsh, and foxy winter down by the railway lines and in the abandoned lots and under-growth. Cats rarely have packs, but we did for a while. There was Aunty Bessy, myself, and Korky, who was a bit dim. We trooped around looking for stuff to eat, to pinch, or even kill. None of us were any good at that. I never got the knack of killing, Bessy is a bit squeamish, and Korky . . . Well, Korky never really understood. When you tried explaining things to him he'd go, "Meep?"

We looked out for each other, against the

other cats, against humans we didn't like, and the foxes and stuff. There's a family of foxes in the railway embankment at the end of Chestnut Avenue. They're very clean and loyal to each other. A decent family, I guess. But they're fierce as anything and, winter 2006, everyone was hungry.

Cold nights, the three of us trooping along in a line. Bessy in the lead, me coming next, little Korky on his bandy legs bringing up the rear. I remember us going along the front gardens and someone opening up the front door just as we were traipsing by. We were caught in the glare as he was putting out the milk bottles late at night.

"Hey!"

It was Paul. Blinking in the lamplight, clutching the milk bottles. Startled by the sight of three cats in convoy, dashing past. He was in his stripy pyjamas, but it wasn't all that late. Certainly not as far as we were concerned. His hair was sticking up and his glasses were smudged. His whole face looked smudgy with concentration, like his mind had been elsewhere all day.

Later I'd find out that's how he was most days. But this was the first time I saw him.

Bessy surged forward, into the hedgerow and the cobbled alley. I shot after her. And Korky should have hurried after me. But

53

the dafty was slower and younger and intrigued by this human putting out the empties. Korky stopped in full glare of light and addressed the human being: "Meep?" In that kind of simpleminded way he has.

Paul's mouth fell open.

But before he could react I shouted, "Ungow!" at Korky to get a move on, and luckily this time he came running after me. Loping along on those silly bandy legs.

Anyhow. That was the first time I saw Paul.

But it was Korky who got the first glimpse inside the house that was about to become my home.

MORE ABOUT OUR GANG

So, that was our gang for a little while.

Korky was still half at home, really. He was only a semirunaway and a part-time stray. He kept going back to his house on Sycamore Avenue, and although Bessy was a bit sardonic about this, it was just as well for us that he did. Korky kept us in supplies during those lean, early days of 2006. He managed to creep in through the cat flap and nab bits and pieces from his owners' larder. He'd lug chicken legs and wings, he'd drag cat pouches and snack packets and make off with them down the lane. And he would share them. He was never greedy. He was always good. Brave and intrepid as well as daft.

The first time I ever tasted smoked salmon in my life was because of young Korky. Somehow one day he got hold of a whole packet of salmon and made off with it. They almost caught him. They called him and called him, but he was away. Into the musty hedges where the humans couldn't follow. He wouldn't dare go back for a while after that.

That was a rare night. Though it did take us a good long while to get the bloomin' packet open. We were all standing round, clawing and scratching at the plastic. We were driven half mad by the heavenly scent of fish and the squidgy feel of it under our paws.

Bessy had made us wait until we were safely in one of the gardens at the back of Chestnut Avenue before we tried to get the salmon open. This was the messiest, most overgrown garden. It was a dark tangle of brambles and overgrown vegetables. But under those dense and dark leaves it was easy to hide out. It was a wilderness filled with a thousand cat scents, going generations back.

This was Smokey's garden. He was the granddad, really, to a whole lot of black-and-white cats round our way. He was as big as the three in our gang put together. He had very green eyes, very long, tattered fur, and his body was basically conical when he sat down. You never saw him move around much. He sat mostly on the front driveway of his owners' house and watched the world go by on the terrace. Other times he came round to this wild back garden and hid out with the likes of us younger ones. We always brought him spoils from our foraging missions, and he was quite pleased about that.

"You three," he said, tutting at us, whenever he saw us hurrying by. "What have you got this time?"

When he saw that on this occasion, it was a whole packet of salmon, he declared that it was reason enough for a little party in the wilderness. A real cat jamboree, as Bessy called it.

As we shredded cellophane and gobbled supper, Smokey was telling us bits of news about the terrace. Nothing had been seen of poor Three-Legged Freddie, who lived next door with the motorbike people. It was rumoured that he'd been in an accident, since he'd lost all road sense. And then there'd been all the fuss about the house on Central Avenue being engulfed in flames last week. It had been a drug den and a flophouse and it had caught fire and gone up in sheets of golden, deadly flame. Several humans and a great many squirrels nesting in the attic and the trees that towered above the house had perished in the brief inferno.

"So?" Bessy shrugged. She could be very

callous when it came to humans, or squirrels. Or other cats, actually. She didn't have much sympathy for anyone besides herself, on the whole.

"The inferno . . ." Korky shuddered, with slivers of salmon hanging out of his mouth. We all thought about that night last week, when the three of us stood watching on the railway embankment as the tall house blazed and the humans ran around, spraying it.

Ungow. I really loved the salmon. It was melt-in-your-mouth stuff. Which is handy when you've got sore gums and only one and a half teeth, like I do.

"Also," continued Smokey wheezily. "There's been burglaries and robberies going on. My owners have been quite worked up about that. They're feeling quite unsafe in their beds at night. That house, two doors down, occupied by that new couple. That was burgled a few nights ago."

"What new couple?" Bessy frowned.

"Those two young gentlemen. They've been in there about a year now. That still counts as new round here. Anyhow, it was a whole gang of kids, getting in through the sitting room window at the back while the two fellas were asleep upstairs. Word has it, one of the fellas went running downstairs at three in the morning and caught them at it!"

We all gasped at the thought of this. If there's one thing all cats know how to do, it's running away from trouble and never towards it. Who was this strange fella in the house two doors down?

Bessy shrugged. "Human beings."

Korky was looking frightened by now. "We're thieves and burglars too, aren't we?"

I knew he was feeling bad for nipping back and nicking stuff from his part-time home. I nudged him to cheer him up.

"That's not the same," Smokey said firmly. "Not at all. You take from the humans what you need to survive. Humans do awful things to each other for no reason at all. Just because they can."

Bessy nudged some more salmon towards the old man, just to quiet him. She didn't like it much when he became philosophical.

We ate companionably for a while, and then we heard yowling from the garden next door. It was the horrible strangled noise of Whisper, the ginger Siamese. She could smell our supper and was furious. We never really talked to her, or anyone else from the motorbike family. Then their Alsatian Ziggy was barking like crazy. But it was just hard lines. We weren't going to give them anything.

Now it was like the whole neighbourhood was waking up. It was midnight, but it was one of those nights when the darkness brightens up. The sky is too light and the stars are somehow a bit multicoloured. The garden was alive with smells and sounds and the music of it all got under our fur and we started to sing. This was one of the things we loved to do together.

Freight trains went rumbling past, and the last London trains came running down the lines into Manchester and the low-flying planes were coming into the airport, just a few miles down the road. When we were singing at the back of Chestnut Avenue, it was like we were at the centre of the whole world.

Sing sing!
Ungow!

Colourful Windows

Korky, it turned out, was very intrigued by the mention of the two young men who'd been burgled. He kept talking about how that was the house where we had walked past the front door and the fella had come out in his pyjamas the other night.

"Huh," scoffed Bessy. "They're not that young, either of them. Midthirties, I'd say."

Bessy was the oldest of our gang — apart from Smokey — and she knew by far the most about humans. She could even tell how old they were! Me, I sometimes even had trouble telling human beings apart.

"I like the way all their windows are lit up," said Korky. "Pink and orange and purple and blue. Each room different. Their house looks so colourful inside. Not like my owners'. Or any other house I've ever seen."

Bessy made a dismissive coughing noise. "They're two men living together, Korky. What do you think of that, eh?"

Korky blinked solemnly. "So?"

Bessy said, "They are gay men. That's what they say."

Korky then had to have the term explained to him. "Why should any of us care about that?" he asked Bessy.

Bessy snapped, "It isn't natural." She picked daintily at her big claws.

"Ungow!" I broke in. "That's what you say, lady. But you go round calling yourself Bessy, and yet you've got the biggest, hairiest pair of bollocks on show that I've ever seen."

She screeched in fury and puffed out her considerable chest. "And what about you, Fester Cat?"

"What about me?"

"You haven't got any bollocks at all! You've been *done*! Your previous owner-but-one took you to the vet and had them RIPPED OFF!"

I squirmed and flinched at the tone of her voice and the horrid mime she was doing.

"That's why you're so little!" she ranted. "That's why you look more like a little girl cat than the middle-aged fella you are!"

She was really losing it. All her teeth were showing, long and pointed. Her eyes were gleaming and her nose was very pink and wet.

"There's no need to get nasty," I muttered.

"Fsssssssstt," she hissed, and started off into the undergrowth. She flicked her tail and we all got a good look at her big balls. Korky and I exchanged a quick glance and almost started to laugh.

I knew really that Bessy was just jealous of my petite physique. She had a proper old bruiser's figure. But there she was, wanting to be known as Bessy. And I've always been so light and trim. I could jump faster, climb higher, dash about quicker. And I can eat just what I want and stay in shape. Silly Bessy. Sometimes I thought she'd never be all that happy in life. She sometimes seemed as if she didn't even want to be happy. Always mithering. That was her.

Maybe it was her bollocks talking? I'd heard that such things could be a proper nuisance.

THE GAY MEN

The next night our little contretemps was as good as forgotten. We met up at midnight and we were mooching in the garden of the house that had turned into an inferno. Bessy had found an interesting patch of stuff, all ashes and clinker and something we couldn't identify.

Then Korky came scrambling over the tall fence. He dashed up to us breathlessly on his bandy legs.

"Shhh," Bessy warned him.

But Korky was too excited. "I've been inside their house! I managed to pay them a visit!"

Bessy turned and did a wee on the cinders and stuff she'd been considering. She scratched about and pulled a nasty face at the little fella. "What? What are you on about, Korky?"

"The gay men! I've been inside their house tonight! I managed to creep throug their kitchen door!"

We both stared at him.

It was a dangerous thing, sneaking into the homes of human beings. Even if you were at your most starving, you never got into a place where you weren't sure of an easy exit. Cat rule book, rule number one. But Korky was dim. He just went traipsing in.

It had been a mild afternoon. The two fellas were out on their back patio. They had a little table and chairs. They had newspapers and books and a big pot of coffee. Music was playing from inside their kitchen. They kept going in and out, fetching things.

Korky was very interested in all of this. He watched them from the long grass of their unkempt garden, considering. They were both the same age and height, really. Both wore glasses. One was smoking cigarettes and he was the one called Jeremy. He had more fur on his face and he was generally grumpier than the other one, who was stuck inside some kind of book, and who was called Paul.

Something delicious was cooking. The smells were drifting out of the kitchen window. Something chickeny, maybe, Korky thought.

While they were going back and forth, immersed in their own things, Korky did a slinky kind of manoeuvre and crossed their patio. Next thing, he was up their back steps in a flash. It was only five steps — and then he was into their kitchen.

"I couldn't take much in at first, but I saw at once that it was pretty big and really messy. Full of all kinds of interesting stuff. And it was chicken they were cooking, in some kind of cream, and bacon, too. It smelled gorgeous."

He closed his eyes as he was telling us this. He really did look a fool.

"What did you do next?" Bessy asked. She seemed shocked at the little cat's temerity.

"I went round every room in the house, having a poke about. And it's true, every room is a different colour. And it's all really cluttered up with things. Stuff that comes from all over the place. Junk and furniture and books and vases and clocks and pictures. It's really, really interesting."

"Fffffffft," said Bessy.

"Anyhow, so I snuck around in there, sniffing round the corners of all the rooms and under cupboards and stuff. Turns out that there's loads of dust and things in there, so I was sneezing a bit and I was scared they'd hear me and chuck me out.

"I heard them coming in from outsid

and they had their dinner at the kitchen table. I was on the staircase. Halfway up. A bit frightened. But still in a kind of trance because of the smell of dinner. I've been a bit starving all day. And earlier today I ate something funny I found under the railway arch. Something mousey and gone bad.

"Then I was even more scared because they banged the back door closed and then I was locked indoors with them. There was no way for me to get out! I listened, and when they finished their meal, they went into the living room and sat down watching the telly. Have you two seen human telly before?"

"Yesss," sighed Bessy crossly. "Of course we have. It's like a little window that they look through and lights come out of it. It calms them down in the evening."

I frowned, because I knew that Bessy hadn't got that quite right.

"I heard the telly and them talking and I thought, Well, they sound okay to me. They don't sound nasty. They don't sound like they'd do any harm to a cat like me."

"Oh, Korky," I said. "You didn't, did you?"

"I did!" He grinned foolishly. "I went in there and I introduced myself to them."

I gasped, same as Bessy. We could both imagine those two human beings sitting in their living room watching their telly and thinking they're alone in their house. When all of a sudden in walks this gangling moggy on bandy legs. Here comes Korky, looking ever so pleased with himself, and wearing his usual lime-green cat collar, if you please.

"Meep!"

He would have said his usual thing to them. The only thing he ever said to human beings.

"Meep!"

I wondered what they thought when they saw he was there.

And I must admit, I felt a bit envious right then.

We sat close together in the rustling dark grass and listened as Korky related the rest of his tale.

"I got too excited. That's what happened. I think I was excited because they looked surprised and then pleased to see me there. They both sat up quickly. One was sitting in the armchair by the window. And the other — Paul — was lying on the settee. They both saw me at once when I bounded into their room and they sat up very quickly. And what a lovely welcome they gave me!

"Of course, I larked about and did some skipping. And then I rolled about on their rug for a tummy tickle and all that stuff.

think they thought I was great.

"And the funny thing was, that Paul looked at me and said, 'It's Korky.' He knew my name! How was that, Fester?"

I shook my head, feeling a bit vexed with him, if I'm honest. Larking about and skipping indeed.

"Anyhow, I started feeling a bit queasy. And then, when I was in the middle of showing off, I realised I had to find a quiet spot. So I went through to their dining room. It's all open plan round their house, you know."

Bessy said, "Oh, Korky, you didn't?"

The little cat looked shamefaced. "I did. I did a horrible poo in the corner of their dining room. Behind a hostess trolley. It was a really sloppy one. But I felt really awful!"

I started to laugh. I couldn't help it. "I bet they were dead chuffed!"

"Plus," said Korky, "I felt a bit sick as well. So I ended up doing a bit of vomit right on top of it to kind of hide it or disguise it. But that was just as bad. In fact, I still feel rotten now, to be honest." He sighed heavily. "I really think I've blown my chances of impressing those two gay men who live there."

Bessy said, "Did they beat you? Did they hase you out?"

"No, no, nothing like that. They looked worried about me, more than anything. They were more concerned about me than their carpet. Which was a horrible biscuit-coloured thing anyway, much the same colour as the mess I'd left. I went to their back door and started scratching at their cat flap, which they'd nailed up. I really wanted to get out again. I was mortified. Paul came and let me out."

Bessy sneered. "Silly young cats. You get yourself all unnecessarily excited and have accidents. They'll never want to see you again now."

"I thought that when they were bringing hot water and rags for their carpet. But they weren't a bit like that. Paul even said, 'See you again, Korky!' when he let me out their back door. But I can't. I couldn't ever go back inside there. I feel so ashamed!"

"Pffffsssst," snorted Bessy, and cuffed the little cat round the lughole.

I must say, I found the whole of Korky's tale quite intriguing. Especially the bit in which Paul somehow knew his name. I mean, how was that even possible?

TREE

I really wasn't showing off. That's not what I'm like at all. But there I was. Halfway up the tallest tree in their garden. I was level with their bathroom window. With everyone's bathroom window, both sides of the terraces. I felt such a fool. I was stuck halfway up a birch tree.

Of course it was all the squirrels' fault. All day they had been chancing it, zooming around the fences and crumbling walls, then bouncing from one tree to another. They were just playing, chasing each other and trying to knock each other down. For some reason today it had got me riled. It was like they thought they owned the whole place and could do just anything they liked. So, up I went. The birch was where one of their nests was — it was easy to see at this time of year. They'd built it out of shreds of old Christmas trees and who knew what else.

What was I thinking I'd do? Shimmy up

there and teach them a lesson? They could be brutal little things. But for some reason that afternoon I just saw red. I dug in my claws and hunched my shoulders and went scampering up the sheer, rugged wall of the tree trunk.

Only when I was two storeys up did I freeze.

I looked across and saw the bathroom lights on in Paul and Jeremy's house. They had a chandelier in there, I was surprised to see. Quite an extravagant thing. Korky hadn't mentioned that. He probably hadn't known what it was. It glittered with crystal light and caught my eye. I hopped onto a slender branch and there I froze again, clinging on for dear life.

From somewhere up above I heard one of the squirrels snicker with amusement.

I tried to ignore it, concentrating on keeping upright. Praying that the branch was strong enough to hold me. We were swaying and bobbing and the drop below was immense.

Now I saw that there was someone in the bathroom window. Paul was there, with a face full of shaving cream, watching. He had seen me, from down the length of the garden. I was mortified. I looked straight ahead and tried my level best to seer nonchalant. I did this stuff every day. This is what tough little cats always did. They climbed out of their comfort zone, and clambered easily back to the ground, one branch at a time.

I peered cautiously at the next branch down. It seemed a very long way away. I loosened the grip of one paw and extended it, airily, downwards. *Swipe. Swipe.* Nope, it wouldn't reach. I was going to have to jump to the next branch and just make sure I didn't miss.

But I think I'll stay here a few moments and gather my concentration and all my energy.

Oh. It's spitting on to rain. And the wind is picking up. Great.

Ungow!

At least that daft Korky and Aunty Bessy aren't here to see my ignoble failure. Oh, why did I go climbing?

When I was younger this kind of height and these sorts of jumps wouldn't have bothered me. They'd be nothing. But it's like something has slipped and changed. It isn't that I've lost my nerve exactly. I've just got to be more careful with myself. I'm skinnier, less fit. This outdoor life has taken its toll.

There's a noise then and I jerk my head

round, making the branch sway violently. It's the crack of a wooden back door, springing open.

It's Paul. In a dressing gown, with wet hair and that foam on his face still. He's hurrying down the steps, across the patio, and down the scrubby grass of their lawn.

What does he think he's going to do? Climb up after me?

I can't have this. I can't have anyone watching me while I'm paralysed with fear. I have to stop being scared. I have to take proper action.

I paw the air again, sweeping my claws about, looking for something I can jump onto.

"It's okay," the human shouts from the ground. "Don't panic! I'll . . . er . . . Um."

He's got his mobile phone out, and I wonder if he's going to phone the fire brigade. That happens, doesn't it? I've seen that happening before. Old ladies call out the firemen when their cats get stuck up trees. In the past, me and my pals have gathered round at a safe distance, laughing our backs off at these kinds of dramas. Well, maybe this is karma.

He isn't phoning anyone. He's taking a picture of me! Trapped up the bloomin' tree! What does he want a picture for?

I grip on, furious. And it's the mocking laughter of the squirrels that makes me take decisive action. I can't hang about like this all day.

I lift up my front paws and leap out onto the air.

Ungow!

It's a wonderfully free feeling for a moment. I'm flying like those squirrels seem to think they can, when they go leaping from branch to branch. Yeah, well, Fester Cat can do it too, squirrels. Even at the age of twelve.

It's a miracle. I make it to the next branch down. I grip hard on to it and give an involuntary cry: "Ungow!" It sounds more like panic than triumph.

Paul takes a step closer. "Fester!"

And at that moment I don't even wonder how he has guessed my name.

The next branch down is closer. It's more substantial too. And it's only a couple of feet higher than the back fence. I can do it. I've almost done it. The wind is crashing about more boisterously now, and I realise that I don't have time to dither up here.

Paul is standing on top of their compost heap. "Jump, Fester!"

So I jump.

One more branch. An awkward twist. A little shriek from me. And a magnificent wriggle in midair. I lash out with my claws and seize hold of the fence at the bottom of the garden. Got it!

And I'm over. I launch myself along the fence, and away. I'm diving into the anonymity of the garden of the burned house beyond. I'm fleeing into that wilderness. I dash away, full of excitement and shame at the same time. My heart is thudding crazily like it hasn't in a long time and what I really need to do is go and lie under a patch of leggy rhubarb I've been hiding out in recently. I'll shelter from the hardening rain under its cool leaves and I'll get my composure back.

But I did it! I survived!

And I proved that I've still got it!

It was nice of that fella to come out to see I was okay. Even if he was no use really.

UP THE BACK STEPS

The days are warmer and brighter. The bulbs on the tall magnolia glow and start to open out. I do a few small climbs and sit resting in the green magnolia branches and watch their house. Then I lie in the long grass and gaze at them from afar.

The boys are on their patio most afternoons now. I hear them saying things about how it's not really warm enough yet, but the sun's too nice to waste. They sit outside in things called "cardies" and scarves and then laugh at themselves for wrapping up like that.

Days go by and it gets warmer still. Spring is coming full force now. My fur is matting together in sweaty clumps and it doesn't feel good. Also, Bessy has given us all fleas. My skin's alive with them. I'm covered in scabs. I'm like one all-over scab because I'm allergic to their bites. I long to roll about on the rough and gritty concrete of the boys' patio.

Then, one day, one Wednesday afternoon, that's exactly what I do. I've had enough of subterfuge and spying.

There's a long, ancient plank of wood acting as a bridge between their lawn and their terrace. It crosses the dip where the old tree used to be before the last owners had it cut down. What I do is, I summon all my bravery and make myself look as nonchalant as I can. Then I put my best feet forward and march primly down the length of that plank, and into their world.

They're both busy reading at their table. It's the brightest part of the day, with the sun pouring golden over the railway embankment. Before I even know I've done it, I've flomped on the warm concrete at their feet.

FFLOMMP.

Headfirst, twisting round, landing on my shoulders and following through with a wriggle and finishing on my back. Paws waggling appealingly, helplessly in the air. I squinch up my eyes and shimmy like mad.

The concrete feels marvelous. It's been storing heat, deep-down heat, for the whole day. The summery warmth has driven the last of the chill away.

It takes a little while for the boys to notice

78

me. By then I've wriggled upright again and I'm having a bit of a delicious clean, pulling at my ears and chewing on my feet.

"Hey," says the one who isn't Paul. "There's your friend."

Paul frowns at me blearily. He has that look I'll soon get to know. The look as if he's coming up for air. He blinks at me. "Yes, that's Fester. Who was stuck up the tree."

Not stuck, I think. Not really stuck. Just chancing his arm. Having an adventure. Dicing with danger.

I flomp again, making it plain I could do with a tickle.

They soon get the message and — lo and behold — they both do my bidding!

Ungow!

More than that, they make a proper fuss of me. I jump up on their table so I can see them eye to eye and they take a good look at me.

"He's so skinny! He looks starved. And hanks of fur are falling out . . ."

"Why's his lip curled up like that? He looks like Elvis!"

I didn't imagine, when I jumped up there, I'd be scrutinised quite so thoroughly. They're fussing over me. When Paul gently touches my face and talks about my lip, I show them my teeth by going:

"Ungow!"

I've only got one and a half teeth. The rest of my mouth is all swollen, bleeding gums. And the weird thing is, I don't even know what happened to me now. It's faded out of my memory. I don't even know when it was. Sometime in my last home, I believe. But the memories of that place — with the dog! — are going away now. And I'm stuck with this mouthful of irksome pain, and a lip which curls over my single fang. It can give me a funny expression sometimes. I look quizzical and piqued at the same time. It's a face I'm doing right now, to these two fellas.

They give me a little dish of milk, which I roll my eyes at. C'mon? A dish of milk? What is this?

"Feel his ribs and his spine. There's nothing to him!"

"And he's covered in sores and scabs . . ."

There's a kind of appalled wonder in their voices. I hadn't realised I was such a woeful specimen. And now I'm starting to wish I'd stayed in the undergrowth. You're not exactly spring bloomin' chickens yourselves, lads!

But like a fool I'm purring. I'm purring like mad. Jeremy's stroking me under my chin. My only weakness. Chinny-chin-chin.

I melt into a kind of trance of wonderful bristly chin-strokiness. I feel like I'm about to . . . to . . .

Fflo — oo-oo — oommmp.

I flomp on their table amongst the papers and books. I'm hopeless! I'm such a sucker for attention! Bessy would laugh in scorn at me today. But luckily the old bag isn't about right now. She's off foraging farther afield. She was off to meet some of the wilder dudes who live closer to the station on Victoria Road. That's what she called them — wilder dudes. Sometimes I don't care much for the company Bessy keeps and the kind of fun she gets up to.

Paul brings me another dish. This is more like it. I can smell what it is as soon as he comes down the back steps. It's cut-up slivers of raw smoky bacon.

I sit up very alert and give each of them my most careful, loving attention. One, two, three. Only three bits?

"I don't want to give him too much in case it makes him sick," he tells the other one.

Jeremy says, "I think he's starving. We can give him more than that."

Yes! Yes! I think, and nudge at his hand. Hard, with my nose.

"His nose isn't very cold and wet," muses

81

Jeremy. "Get him some more food!"

Well, I wolf a handful more of the most wonderfully savoury, moist bacon. And then suddenly I'm alert and ready to go. I hop off the table.

"See you later, losers!" I cry, though I don't mean it nasty.

They're okay, those two.

I Decide to Adopt

That night in the wild garden, I catch up with Bessy — who looks shifty — and Korky. The littlest of us is thoughtful and a bit worried. It turns out he's been back at his old home again. His owners were delighted to have him back for the day, and made a real fuss of him.

"I was pampered," he tells us. "The older one, the mother-kind-of-person, she wept all over me and said how much they had all missed me."

Bessy growled, because she could see what was coming next. "You're going to move back in. You're going to leave our gang and become a house cat again. A spoiled and stuck-up housey-house cat."

Korky threw himself down on the oily, dirty ground. He was really miserable. "They're moving away," he said. "My family are moving to another town. Quite soon. That's what I learned today. And so I have to make a decision. I can't be a half-time homey anymore." He sighed. Suddenly that little cat in the lime-green collar sounded as if he had grown up.

"Whatever," growled Bessy, monumentally unimpressed with Korky's quandary. "Just you remember who your friends are, eh? Who looked after you and showed you the ropes. It was us! Us, young Korky!"

"I know," Korky moaned pitifully. "And I'm very grateful, Aunty Bessy. But really, I do think I belong with them. And inside a proper home and all . . ."

I was very quiet that night. I didn't want to say anything about my visit to the two boys.

Luckily, Bessy was more concerned with bragging about her own escapades. She had been in the Rat Runs under the railway platforms at Levenshulme station. It was one of the things that rough gang from Buckhurst Road loved to do. It was one of their initiation rites. To send new members into the steel cage of the Rat Runs, to goad the wildest and biggest of the railway rodents into fighting. It was a nasty, cruel, grisly business and there was always a lot of nastiness and blood. Even from Chestnut Avenue we could sometimes hear the squeals and screeches of the Buckhurst

Gang's initiations.

It was obvious Bessy was getting into very bad company. "That lot — all those immigrant cats — they need to know who's boss round here. They need to understand that us lot were here first of all."

She was always so concerned about status, was Bessy. Fighting and one-upmanship and standing her ground. I think I was discovering about myself — at the grand old age of twelve — that I would give just about anything in order to have a much quieter life than the one Aunty Bessy craved.

We ate stolen chicken under the moonlight in the desolate garden of the house that had burned down. And it was one of the last times the three of us were all together.

The following afternoon, I returned to the house of those boys. This time they didn't need persuading too much to bring me some bacon. As I sat on their table I actually drooled. I could get used to this, I thought.

In a moment of inspiration, I hopped off that table and scampered up those back steps.

Then I was into their kitchen, just like Korky had been sometime before.

I met Paul halfway as he was coming out with the dish of soft bacon bits.

"Oh, you followed me inside, Fester!" he said, grinning. He set down the dish just where he stood on the bare wooden boards of the kitchen.

"Ungow!" I said.

At Home

It was a long summer, and I spent many of my days with them in their garden. I stretched as long as I could go on the concrete patio, and absorbed as much sun as possible. Then when it got too much I would sit in the tall, untended grass among the purple flowers. I listened and I watched, and I got to know the boys.

Their families lived in other towns and sometimes they would make trips elsewhere for days on end.

Those weekends I'd be back to my normal life, and Bessy would be sarcastic. "Have your friends left you, then?" she'd sneer.

She was looking tougher than ever. Muscular and angry. She also smelled of living wild in abandoned lots. She smelled of the musky sprays of many different cats. She smelled of blood.

Korky was increasingly apologetic. He brought more and more elaborate gifts of food for his homies, culminating in a whole packet of wonderful Parma ham.

Bessy didn't turn up to his farewell feast.

"She's disgusted with me, chew chew, chew," he said.

"She just isn't a very domesticated cat," I told him. "She has to do her own thing, chew, chew, chew, and you've gotta do yours, Korky."

"We're moving away to Cheshire!" he said excitedly. "I don't know where it is, but it sounds nice. They're talking about being in the countryside, chew, chew, chew."

"You'll love it," I said. "You'll soon forget us and everything here in Limefield and beside the railway tracks."

"I don't want to forget, Fester, chew, chew, chew."

"That's how it works. We have to move on into new bits of life. Just the way I can hardly remember, now, the first house I lived in, or why I left, chew, chew, chew. I'm having trouble sometimes remembering my second home, too, where they got the dog and they didn't want me anymore."

Korky looks at me like he feels sorry for me, but he needn't. Because I have a new plan, and a new life in mind.

September brings cooler mornings. There's a real bite to the wind that comes roaming over the back gardens. Still, the days are long and the sun still comes in the late afternoon, leaving hot little traps of warm to sit in. The boys are still there. Paul sits with lots of books and papers. I hop on the table and sit amongst them. I sit on what he's reading and nudge at him when he looks like he needs a distraction.

That music of theirs spills out onto the terrace from the kitchen. Spangling, infectious music. Disco music. Odyssey, Barry White, Baccara. I get to know all the silly names.

They feed me every day now. I think they feel responsible. As if, once they started giving me food, they had to keep giving, as if I had no other way to sustain myself. They wonder how, with one and a half meagre teeth, I could kill or chew anything. So they bring out a single pouch of fancy cat food when I appear each day in the late afternoon.

Don't get me wrong, I'm not turning my nose up at it. How could I? I just find it touching that they have started to feel responsible for my upkeep.

They squeeze the contents of the fancy pouch into a plastic dish and sit it before me, and I must say it makes me feel quite luxurious, having this kind of stuff each day. I'm developing a taste for these chunks of beef in gravy, fish in jelly.

Pou-ches. It's like a magic word in my head. It chimes in the middle of the afternoon. Ungow! Time to check out those daft lads and their Pou-ches.

Also, I'm quite casual now about spending time with them in their house.

When it rains in the evening they ask me in and I spend time with them in their living room. They spend quite a lot of time in front of the television. They treat it like the magic window Bessy described. They see all sorts of marvelous things in there, and are quite hooked. They sit still, tense and fretting. They laugh until they cry. They shout back at some of the things people say in there and the evenings are quite busy and noisy as a result.

I sit on the floor, and once or twice in recent weeks, I have made a few tentative forays onto laps. First Paul, who sits the most still, and then Jeremy. Awkward, at first. They sat as if they were scared of dropping me. That suited me fine as I made sure I was comfy. I lay there where I could see this telly of theirs and listened to all the voices and watched the colours play. I did that kneading thing with my paws because they seemed to love that.

I remember first falling asleep on Paul's knee. I woke with a jump. For an instant I had no idea where I was. Then I did. I was okay. I was safe. I was at home.

I lay on his chest as he lay flat on the sofa. My nose was almost pressed against his nose. My paws were under my chin, kneading his shirt. I purred quite a bit. Sing sing.

"He's singing to me," Paul told the other one. "He's going 'Hoo-ha hoo-ha.' "

Each night, before midnight, when they went to bed, they'd put out the milk bottles and lift me up and put me out at the front of the house. I think they fondly imagined that I'd go off hunting through the night or something. I didn't want to disabuse them of the notion that I did such things, so off I marched, gamely down the terrace, wondering where I might find a nice spot to sleep.

In the morning I'd be back, beside the full bottles of milk, waiting on the doorstep.

"Ungow!"

It became my routine, in all weathers. Even when it was fine I was keen to get back indoors. Their cushions and settees had my scent on them. I actually liked eating indoors. Now I preferred it to eating out.

Soon, especially when it rained heavily, like it did that autumn, I found myself scratching at their door. I don't remember ever doing anything so needy or pathetic before. But there I was. *Scratch, scratch.* Let me in.

I did smelly sprays either side of their front door, killing bushy plants in urns and leaving everyone with no doubt that from now on this was Fester's house.

One night when it came to bedtime I slunk away and hid myself in a lovely dusty corner, between a cupboard and a radiator. They gave up looking for me and went to bed. I was delighted to be locked in with them.

I prowled that house like I owned the whole thing. I went down into the cellar, which was as big as the whole house, and held brilliant, damp-smelling cardboard boxes crammed with inexplicable things. I marked it and went back upstairs and padded about on the kitchen table and all the surfaces. I even sat in the sink, licking a dish they'd baked fish in.

In the middle of the night I realised I had nowhere to go to the loo. I'd miscalculated and I felt silly as Korky. Korky doing his skipping and showing off and then getting caught short.

What I did, I produced the tidiest piece of poo I could manage. I laid it very carefully, precisely, with as little mess as possible, bang in the middle of their stairs. Halfway up. There was no missing it. I wasn't being like some dirty cat and just hiding it away. I was presenting this poo as a plain and straightforward message. It said, "Okay, guys. If I'm living here and conducting all my business, day and night, under your roof, then we need some arrangements sorting. I'll need a tray, or whatever. Ungow!"

When Paul came downstairs first and saw the poo he understood at once what I was saying. He wasn't dismayed or worried at the sight of that small piece of poo. He later on got Jeremy to take the boards off their cat flap, so I could come and go as I pleased, but no dice. I don't even know why, but there was no way I was sticking my head through that thing. It was some gut level thing I had about it.

Maybe I'd had a bad experience with one in the past? That was Paul's best guess. Maybe something even I couldn't remember. Maybe I was repressing a bad memory of a cat flap? Well, whatever, I'd go with that. But I was never gonna use the horrible thing.

They bought me a litter tray.

And guess what? This tough homeless street cat was proud. I was actually proud of this thing.

It was lilac and they filled it with stuff that smelled of pine. Stuff that was good for scratching in and kicking up over the edge of the tray. The best thing was, they placed it in their huge bathroom, between their claw-foot tub and the tall window that overlooked the garden. In their very own bathroom, under the Venetian chandelier, right near the toilet where they both did their own business.

I felt honoured. And I really felt like part of the family now.

I did my first poo in the tray that night and hurried downstairs where they were watching their precious *Doctor Who*. It was a show I was getting to love watching with them. They had friends round with glasses of wine. There was laughter. Good. Here were some more of their friends I hadn't had a good look at yet.

I trotted nonchalantly round the corner and into their midst. "Mow," I announced, and got the message across. "Something for you, upstairs, fellas. Something you might want to deal with." And, "Hiya, everyone else! I'm Fester Cat!"

THE SPANISH WOMAN

It's a few days later and I'm having a loll on the roof of their car. They've got this silver Škoda parked on their front yard and it's in the perfect position for a bit of a lie in the morning. From here I can see the other cats go past on the terrace. I'm two doors down from Smokey, and he watches me with an appraising eye.

"Settling down at last, Fester Cat." He nods approvingly. I think he's glad I'm not tearing about the place like Bessy is. Come to think of it, we haven't seen her round here for more than a week. Last time, she said we were going all "suburban" and "bourgeois." I don't know where she's getting these new words from, but she can just get lost. I don't care if I'm suburban. I'm comfy, so, whatever.

The cats belonging to the motorbike people across the alleyway come by to have a look at me, atop my Škoda. That sly, whingeing Siamese, and Three-Legged Freddie, who lopes around in circles and loops. His brown fur is shaggy with tangles and knots and he reeks of widdle. "I've got four legs actually, ta very much," he snorts. "I just had a big stroke and one of my back ones went wonky. Which is why — huff huff — I go round in friggin' circles, innit?"

We've all watched him trying to get across the road, spiraling and looping the loop, huffing and puffing away while the cars honk their horns. He's all right, though, Freddie. Bit of a scrounger. When I was eating al fresco on the boys' patio he used to come galumphing by and I had to warn him.

Uuuuuuuunnnnnnnnnnngggggggggggggggg-ggoooooooooooooooooooooow.

He got the message, and ambled away, pirouetting like a stinky ballerina.

I'm watching him go by this morning and then someone calls out. A human. A woman! I jump and turn round.

She's standing by the car. An older woman in a beige mac and dyed curly hair. Suddenly alarm bells go off. I know this woman. I think I like her.

"Paula?" she asks. Steps closer. "Isn't it Paula?"

"Ungow?" I say warily. I stand up, stretch, and move a little closer to where she's holding out her hand to touch my face. Yes, her scent is familiar.

"It is you, Paula?" she says.

Then, all at once I feel ashamed. It's the woman who thinks I'm a girl.

She's my previous owner. The one from over the road, who I ran away from, last year.

Later that evening, when we're all in the kitchen and there's disco music on, I'm getting my five o'clock tea and Paul is cooking. He's opening a bottle of wine and telling Jeremy all about the outrage of the Spanish woman.

Barry White is singing, "My First, My Last, My Everything," which is fast becoming one of my favourite songs.

"Is she Spanish, though?" Jeremy asks, frowning. "I don't think she is . . ."

It turns out Paul was watching the whole unfolding scene in the front garden from his tiny study, directly above the front door. He sat there holding his breath as the woman approached me.

"That's the thing," he's saying now. Wooden spoon dripping meat sauce in one hand, glass of Côtes du Rhône in the other. "I thought she was going up to Fester and saying, 'Hola! Hola!' like she was Spanish, and she thought he was Spanish too."

"No, no," Jeremy says. "If it's the woman I think it is — in the beige mac, lives across the way — she's not Spanish."

"Well, that's how it turned out," says Paul. "Because when I went down there it turned out that she wasn't saying 'hola' at all. She was saying 'Paula.' "

Jeremy frowns. "Paula?"

"She was calling Fester 'Paula.' I honestly thought she was going to kidnap him."

"But he's a boy cat!" Jeremy cried. "Not a girl! How dare she? He *is* a boy, isn't he?"

I kept on eating, fascinated by their conversation. I must admit, though, I was horrified having that woman shouting a girl's name at me in the front street.

"I went downstairs," says Paul. "I flung open the front door and thundered outside. I asked if I could help and she looked at me, a bit regretfully. Then she said, 'I am very glad that Paula is living with you now. You and your partner. I am happy that she has found a new home. She used to be our cat, you see. Until she ran away last year. We took her in as a stray too. But she left us last year because we got a dog, you see. And she wasn't very happy being in the house with our dog.' "

And all at once the memory of that horrible, slavering beast comes back to me.

And the dreadful feeling of having no-where to go. Of having to pack up my metaphorical goodies and get out of there.

"Paula!" said the woman both Paul and I had thought of — briefly — as the Spanish woman. For a few awful moments we both thought she was going to take me back to her house that smells of dog.

But she wasn't. She smiled sadly and said, "So, I'm happy that she is yours now. She is a free spirit. She has chosen to be with you! Good-bye! Good-bye, Paula!"

Then she fiddled self-consciously with the collar of her beige mac, and picked up her shopping bags again, and turned to hurry off to her own smelly house.

Phew.

I looked at Paul. "Ungow?"

"It's all right, Fester," he said, and grabbed me, carrying me back inside the house. "You're with us now. Not with some Spanish woman who thinks you're a girl."

And now in the kitchen, Jeremy's laughing and pleased. "So, he's ours now! We should see about getting him to the vet's and checked out. And getting him chipped and registered."

I'm not sure I like the sound of that, entirely. But the boys are in a jubilant mood, suddenly. They're talking about making things official. I take a short running jump and spring onto the kitchen table, just as Jeremy pours himself a glass of his pink wine and they clink their glasses together. The toast is, "To Fester Cat!"

A Boy

At the vet's I'm not happy. I'm pretty mortified, actually.

The vet is a young woman. Quite nice.
Very professional.

It's in a little shop on Levenshulme High
Street, which I know from my very oc-
casional visits as a stray is mostly discount
stores, bookmakers, and kebab shops. It was
the kebab shops behind my reason for foraging here — along with Bessy — during the
bleaker weeks of winter.

Now here I am, being a special patient at
the vet's. They're giving me injections as I
stand on the smooth table. I'm trying my
best to be good. She brings out clippers like
the ones Jeremy does his face with and they
shave patches of fur so they can get at me
with the needles.

"It's the hairdresser," Jeremy says, ruffling
my fur. "You're getting a new hairdo."

I humour him, submitting to all these

medical things. I gather this is all good stuff, to stop me getting ill, but it's still a bloomin' liberty. Especially first thing in the morning. I'm trying to be brave and hard and all. But I let the side down by trembling. I give in to the shakes. I let a bit of wee out as well.

The lady vet tells Jeremy that I've got fleabites and I've had a rough time living outdoors. Well, tell us something we don't know. She rambles on a bit, but I don't really listen. She goes on about the microchip thing, and Jeremy's agreeing. Then she's fussing with the scruff of my neck. There's a squeezing sensation, then something sharp and suddenly it's done. Whatever it is.

Jeremy says, "We had a visit from the previous owner, who says she's happy with the new arrangement. But the woman seemed to think this cat was a girl."

I was lying there on the table, glaring up at them both.

"Oh dear, no," says the lady vet, pulling me about. "Fester Cat is most definitely a boy. If you look here, you will see his penis."

Ungow! What?! I've never been so embarrassed in all my life. Some young woman talking about my . . . doings in front of one of my new gentleman owners. Jeremy is laughing. "I can't see it," he says, and now I feel even worse. Now I'm even wishing I had great big bollocks like Bessy. Oh, I just want to go home and hide myself away in the garden.

"Fester seems to me to be between ten and twelve," says the lady vet. "He's been neutered, at quite a young age, which is why he's so petite. He's a very handsome cat indeed."

Well, she needn't think she can start sucking up to me now.

I keep quiet for the rest of the visit as they talk fleas and dietary requirements and other stuff. If Jeremy and Paul are looking after me from now on, just let them remember all the complicated stuff. And let me get on with just being a cat. A mature gentleman cat. That's what I am. And a very handsome one at that. Ungow!

Once home, Jeremy relates all this to Paul. They're in the kitchen, with the back door open and disco music on. It's their meeting place, I have realised. It's the middle of the house.

Through the door I can see the sun is gentle on the back garden. On the coloured leaves and the mellow red brick of the houses.

Paul cracks up laughing at Jeremy's penis

story. And he seems very pleased indeed to hear about the microchip.

He tells me, "That means you can never lose us, Fester. If ever we're separated they can take you in and read the chip. And it will give them our names and address. They'll just look at their computers and know that you belong with us, and they'll bring you straight back home. You're with us now, Fester Cat. Forever now!"

And to me that sounds a lot like, "Ungow! Ungow!"

SLEEPING

It took some doing and a lot of scratching at their bedroom door, but they got the message. Now I sleep on their bed at night. They should have realised earlier. They made up a little basket for me downstairs with soft blankets and stuff. And that's fine for afternoon naps and evenings, I suppose

At night, though, I've got to be on top of that bed. There's no two ways about it.

Paul's side, it has to be. Jeremy is jumpy and moves around way too much. He turns over in his sleep so elaborately, so noisily. Anyone nearby would be thrown off. Paul's side is best as he lies almost unnaturally still and makes lots of room for me. Over the weeks and months I've been training him to give me more and more of his side of the bed, gradually yielding it up until he's sleeping diagonally and I've got a nice wide spot about halfway down. Right where the sun creeps in at dawn.

Sometimes I can get Paul to sleep still enough so that I can lie across his knees and balance there at full stretch all night long. Sometimes when he bends his legs correctly I can shelter in the crook of his knees, which forms just the right shape for curling up in.

I like their room. There's lots of bookcases going up to the ceiling and the books smell interesting. They smell of every house the boys have ever lived in, and so, even without reading, I understand some of their history.

Paul always goes to bed earliest. He sits up under lamplight with the covers pulled over his lap, usually with a range of books scattered about him. I let him get settled there and then I come sauntering in, quite casually. I poke my head round the open door and act surprised to see him there.

"Mow?" I ask. It's best to ask politely.

Often he's so stuck into reading he doesn't even notice. That's my cue to take a running jump and pounce. I land nimbly on the duvet right in front of him.

"Ungow?"

I pad luxuriously over the wonderfully crushy crinkly feel of the duck-down duvet. Also, the fake satin of the blue blanky feels like heaven under my paws. It makes a very satisfying sound when I click it with my claws.

Then Paul notices me. He pats the covers and I come to lie across his knees, or his lap, or if he's lying down, on his chest. I try to wriggle between his face and the book.

Sing sing.

As he reads he strokes between my ears (making the fur stand up into a "hairdo") and all around my ears. The very edges of my ears are highly sensitive and feel papery and shivery. I purr like mad when he does this. Also, he's cleverly discovered that I adore having both my ears smoothed down backwards. He calls this "mammy cat ears" because he imagines it reminds me of having a mother cat and how she'd clean m with great big swipes of her tongue over my small skull. Well, obviously I don't remember stuff like that, but "mammy cat ears" feels terrific anyway and I squinch my eyes with joy when he does it.

In the early days I'm almost embarrassed at how easily I'm won over by these things. But it's true. A bit of attention and I'm quite helpless. Stroking under the chin and the Special Spot above my collarbone. He holds my front paws too, absentmindedly, his attention still on his book. He puts the tip of one finger at a time under my paw and gets me to clench my claws around it. This feels wonderful, his pulse warming the chilly pads of my feet. He doesn't even mind that my feet are sometimes stinky.

He knows just how to sit and fuss about with me. Not too much, because that's aggravating. But a little bit of patting and tickling doesn't come amiss. It's been a long time.

When he dozes off, sometimes I do too. I'm going singsing and breathing slower and slower. I can feel our breathing at the same time. This should be impossible since he's a huge, galumphing human being and I'm quite a small cat. His lungs must be so much bigger than mine. But when we both ⁀igh our deepest, most contented sigh, it's at just the same time and lasts just as long. The first time it happens I think he's copying me and taking the Mickey. I open my eyes to check and he's just smiling at me.

Round about this time I teach him to wink. We were playing a game to do with narrowing our eyes as we lay there face-to-face. Smaller and smaller, outstaring each other. Seeing who would close their eyes fully and trust the other one completely. In order to throw off his concentration I gave him a rakish wink and he shouted out in laughter. He called out to Jeremy to come and see.

"Fester winked at me!"

"What?" shouted Jeremy, who was at his computer in the room next door, wreathed in cigarette smoke and frowning at the screen.

"Ungow," I said, because Paul was moving about too much.

Well, of course I didn't do the winking thing again. I'm not some performing cat. I would bide my time till I showed off that particular skill again.

FIT

My fleabites cleared up. All those nasty scabs dropped off. I no longer itch. My skin doesn't feel flaky, swollen, achy like it did. I'd become so used to that, and scratching at myself with overgrown claws. I'd started to think it was normal. I was used to my fur feeling matted and greasy. All of that stuff I'd accepted as just how things were going to be.

But they're not. Everything has changed. These cold little drops of medical stuff they put on my neck, under my collar, and the injections and pills — all these things have done their work. Though I squirmed and tried to run away, it's been worth it in the end.

I feel marvelous. I feel sproingy and new.

My nose is cold and wet.

I feel less mithered and grumbly. I know I was getting a bit like that. I was becoming middle-aged and irked all the time. But it was just because I was uncomfortable.

Now I want to run about at top speed and roll on the ground and flomp all over the place and show off.

I've put on weight too. All those pouches, all those little snacks. All those little shreds of bacon and ham. I'm filling out, Jeremy says.

And I feel good.

When Korky comes to say good-bye he looks amazed by my transformation.

"You're so glossy!" he says. "The white on your belly and chest and your socks — it's gleaming!"

"I've been looked after," I say proudly.

We're in my new backyard, on the patio together. It's a chilly autumn morning and Korky's hopped over the crumbling brick wall. Full of his news. His people are at last doing their move to the country and to Cheshire. Far away. He has come by to tell me he'll never see me again.

"You're a good lad, Korky," I tell him. He looks pleased by this. He is more settled and calm. Less flighty and daft. I've known him since he was a long-legged bandy scrap of a thing and I've seen him become a sensible grown-up cat in that time. Home life suits him, it turns out. Much more than being a stray. And I've been discovering th it suits me too.

"I wish I could find Bessy," he says sadly. "She always looked out for me. She protected me when I was little. But I've been up Windsor Road and Buckhurst Road. I've been as far as I dare go. Even as far as Albert Road. But I can't see her anywhere."

I sigh. Wherever she is, Bessy is missing out. I don't suppose she even knows we're about to lose our daft little friend. "I'll tell her for you," I promise Korky. "I'll say that you went to Cheshire and you were happy and that you sent her your fondest regards."

"My love!" he says. "I send her my love. And I hope she'll be happy one day."

In his own way Korky has said something I've always been vaguely aware of. Bessy is never really contented. Always scrapping, always vexed.

I go with Korky to see Granddad Smokey, who sits in his mud pile at the front of his house. He goes very solemn and philosophical. "You're going a very long way away, Korky Cat. Didn't I always say you would, one day?" Korky listens very carefully as the old sage goes rumbling on and on. Advice and admonitions. Then we both become aware that he's snoring. He's sitting quite still like a grand old heap of grey fur and snoring noisily.

"Bye, Smokey." Korky grins and goes loping off on his bandy legs.

That sneaky Whisper has come to say an actual friendly good-bye, maintaining her distance all the same. And Three-Legged Freddie is going round in wobbly circles on the path, huffing out his farewells. He's getting dried and crumbly horse chestnut leaves stuck in his tatty fur. "We'll see you again, huff huff, young Korky! What goes around comes around, remember!"

But I think Freddie is wrong. This is it. Korky is going a very long way away. He won't be coming back here again.

I wonder if Three-Legged Freddie has gone doo-lally? Or is it because he's doomed to go round in wobbly circles all the time? Is that why he thinks everything and everyone just goes round and round?

When I say ta-ta at the corner of Chestnut Avenue to the cat who's felt like a younger brother, he races gleefully back to his house. They're busy packing boxes in there, the humans, and I know Korky likes nothing more than messing with cardboard boxes. I hope he doesn't get *too* excited.

The last moments we spend together are happy ones.

So. There goes Korky, I think, scampering my way home.

Our gang is split up altogether now.
And I am a house cat once more.

ALBERT

One night not long after that they had a
friend visiting. One I didn't know yet. All I
knew, as soon as he came in, was that I
didn't want to sit on his lap. I just know, as
soon as I get a look and a sniff of a person.
This one was bony and angular. He was
dressed in a smart suit that smelled like
static electricity. They called him Albert,
and it turned out that they knew him from
the last town they lived in, before I knew
them.

They gave him steak and chips. I sat right
at the edge of the kitchen table to watch
Paul frying it dry both sides in the pan for
scant minutes and then sliding it into the
oven. It was one of my favourite things that
he cooked. He'd always keep aside a small
piece of the meat. He'd chop it up fine. Just
enough to chew on. The pink juices would
make me feel dizzy as I sat there with them,
eating this stuff.

"Oven chips!" Albert guffaws, surveying their kitchen. Everything in the kitchen was wooden and old. The fittings and furnishings and even the lighting was pink and orange. I could see that Albert didn't approve. "After I travel all this way to see you, you feed me oven chips?!"

He watched Paul putting out dinner, and then he started reacting in mock horror to the missing chunks of plaster on the walls, and the ruined bit of ceiling where the old shower room had fallen through (luckily before I moved in).

"Good God," Albert said. "You're living in a hovel. Just look at this place. You've lived here for over a year now. Almost two. Why haven't you had it seen to? Why hasn't Jeremy done his famous DIY on it? It's not a bad little house, this, but it's all wrong. You've filled it with all your clutter, just like the last place."

Paul shrugged and smiled, and I could tell he was carefully biting his tongue. He melted butter in the hot frying pan and made a peppery gravy for the steaks. I turned to watch Albert through narrowed eyes.

We sat in the dining room to eat. We had candles going in the silver holders and logs burning in the little fireplace. Albert looked slightly startled when, a few minutes into their meal, my head popped up in one of the spare places. I don't think he was expecting me to sit properly in a chair of my own.

Albert was in the middle of a long, complicated story about his new job. It turned out that he was moving to Manchester. This trip wasn't just to visit the fellas, it was also all to do with his new post at one of the universities. He had been put in charge of something important-sounding called research.

"I will be measuring outcomes and outputs," he said, smacking his lips with relish. He pushed his chips to one side of his plate. "I'll be the one at the top, making academics such as yourself, Paul, accountable for describing the progress — or otherwise! — of your research and evaluating its excellence and worthiness. I will be measuring the global impact of the things you and your fellow academics are writing."

Paul looked at him. "But that sounds like an awfully busy job. How will you be able to read everyone's books in time?"

"Read?" Albert looked mystified, and then appalled. "Indeed not. I won't be reading any such stuff. I shall evaluate the research outcomes for value and then construct th virtual Grid of Excellence, which will demonstrate their worth. Or otherwise."

He went on like this for some time about his job.

It sounded terrible.

Paul's attention strayed — I could tell. Jeremy seemed to know exactly what Albert was talking about. He started telling Albert that he had got the whole thing wrong and didn't really comprehend the underlying issues. Jeremy then asked Albert a lot of questions and they made Albert's face turn dark pink like the inside of the steak.

I was up on the table eating more little bits of that steak.

I was nibbling from Paul's finished plate. They were beautiful blue plates. Apparently they were Jeremy's parents' wedding dinner service. I was, at this point, starting to appreciate the finer things in life. Hark at me! Having steak off blue vintage dinner plates!

Albert let out a squawk of outrage. "You let that stray animal onto the table?!"

Paul says, "Yes, of course we do."

I lean forward to nuzzle him, nudging my whole face against his and bumping our noses together. I hurry over and do the same for Jeremy. Don't want him feeling left out. I know I'm overdoing it but I want this Albert person to feel the full force of a cat snub.

"Oh my God, you're kissing him! You're letting your bloody cat literally kiss you at the dinner table!"

Albert looks as if he's about to pass out. He dabs his face with a fuchsia napkin and tosses it down. He looks really flustered.

"You pair get yourselves a pet and look what's happened to you!" He stares beadily at my two boys and then he says, "Unmet needs, I call it. That's what a therapist would say. That's what this is. You've both got issues and unmet needs!"

BATH TIME

Paul lies in the deep claw-foot bath and sings every morning: *"It's bath . . . time . . . do-do do-do . . . do-do . . ."*

He bathes in the late morning, after a few hours at his desk. When he sings that song he knows I'll have followed him. I'll be sitting in a patch of sunlight on the carpet right behind him. I lie down flat and listen to his song:

"It's bath . . . time . . . Fester the Cat
and . . . Paul . . ."

He's splashing about with bubbles and stuff and it's my cue to do a little cleaning up too. He gets a real kick out of turning round and seeing me performing my ablutions just as he's doing his. Licking my haunches and my legs, holding them up like a ballerina, one front paw hooked around a back knee. The one that always makes him laugh is when I lick my chest and try to go higher up my neck and it's all too close to reach. I flick my tongue about like crazy and roll my eyes and I do it just to hear him laugh. He laughs too when I do the serious business of licking my bum, and then he says I'm on the phone to my pals.

This morning I'm still thinking about that bloke Albert's visit last night and what it all meant. He left quite late, calling a taxi to his city centre hotel, and my boys waved him off. The rain was coming down and I stood looking through their legs at the dark street. I wondered about slinking out for the night, like the old days, and visiting some old haunts. But really, it looked way too cold and wet. The last train from London hooted and rumbled by and I hurried back indoors.

Albert's visit is still on Paul's mind too as he sploshes about in the tub. "Unmet needs, indeed," he says. "Who'd know more about those than Albert? Ha!" He's calling to Jeremy, who's in his study, doing work e-mails.

I must say, Jeremy seems to have a very boring job. It involves lots of long and complicated e-mailing, which means endless typing of very small words into tight boxes on the computer screen, and then zipping them off into the ether. Then they come back later, full of more things to reply to. Jeremy sits at his desk sometimes getting crosser and crosser, smoking ever more cigarettes. Often he gets on the phone, pacing about the paper-strewn confines of his room, talking in that loud voice of his. Often he's laughing, but other times he's sounding outraged or aggrieved. Either way it's not very relaxing for a little cat to be around. Though, I must admit, his supremely messy study has some tantalisingly dusty corners for hiding in.

"Anyhow," Paul's going on. "We *all* have unmet needs, don't we? That's like . . . the whole human condition, isn't it? Bloody hell. I wish I'd thought of that last night when your friend was being so bloody snooty about us having a cat and spoiling him a bit. I mean, what's wrong with making a fuss of him? Fester's great. And he's had a tough life up till now, the vet said so. He deserves to be spoiled by us!"

Ah yes. That's true. Mr. Joe the vet. The man vet is who I get seen by mostly these days. Not that there was anything wrong with the young woman, even if she did talk quite casually about my penis. But I prefer Mr. Joe. We're on first-name terms. He's ry calmly in control. He did all my injec-

123

tions and stuff no bother, and he has a re-assuringly firm hand.

Jeremy mumbles something from his room. Something about Albert not being *his* friend in particular. He's *both* their friends.

I feel like telling them what I know about friendship. What cats say about such things. It's like, well, you know, over time and distance friendships can change. They must change. You lot were all friends together a few years ago, when you all lived in the same street, in the same town. But you can't expect that to go on forever. Time gets in the way. Long distance gets in the way. People change too. They develop new friends, new interests, new habits. They learn to want different things.

We're in an ever-shifting cosmos, guys! Don't you realise that? How can everything stay constant?

I'm a cat, you see. I understand this stuff. Cats live in the here and now. We are opportunists and chancers. We are pragmatists. We change all the time.

That's what the nine lives thing means.

It doesn't mean that we're immortal, though some of us seem to have the luck of the devil.

No, it means that we are used to the id

that we must change and adapt and become other people sometimes.

And this means that at certain points we must turn our backs on who and what we used to be.

All of this wisdom is what Bessy taught me about being a cat. Bessy and Smokey and all those other, older fellas. It's the received lore of cats round here.

So, having grown up with that, I can kind of see where this Albert is coming from. I understand why he seemed so different in the boys' eyes. He was colder, harsher, snobbier than before. He was keen on there being a pecking order, on looking down on people, on looking out for number one. And maybe that's what he's had to become, for his new life, his new job. This new phase of his life.

One thing I know for sure. Cats are like that because of fear. Because they know they are fundamentally alone. They have no true loyalty because they only look after themselves. And that's what this Albert is like. I can tell.

"He really thinks he's *it* these days," Paul grumbles. "I mean, he always thought he was something before . . . But now!"

Oh, who am I kidding? I was never any ood at all that ruthless feline stuff. I was never all that good at adapting to circumstances and turning my back. I could never quite be like Bessy — or even Korky. I have always been the same. I'm Fester.

I will be loyal to those who are kind to me. And I'll always feel bruised and upset when things are changed around me, out of my control, and the world moves on. In the past I have been turned against, I've been shunned and blanked and treated quite differently by those I thought of as friends. I could never get used to it. I always used to think, Why can't things stay the same? Why can't people just stay nice?

Ungow.

Deep thoughts for a Tuesday morning.

It's eleven o'clock. Our minds are supposed to be at their keenest at this point in the week. Paul read that somewhere and told me all about it. Hmm. Perhaps it's true. I'm feeling pretty sharp just now.

He dries himself quickly and dresses all in a rush. It's always the same when he's been in a deep bath, thinking things over. Now he's dashing about and I know he's had a series of ideas going off in his head like firecrackers. This seems to be how he works. Lots of thoughtful lolling about then sudden, frenetic activity. He can't get to his desk quick enough.

126

He dresses in very faded old jeans, a black T-shirt, and a crumpled blue oxford shirt. One of his usual, ultracasual outfits. I approve of the universal sloppiness of his dress. All his clothes are old and have been washed and worn a million times. He's all soft, crumpled cotton — that's him. Even when he gets new clothes it's like they immediately become frayed and old within days of his first wearing them. He does something to them — it's like magic. Everything he touches becomes comfy.

Something a cat can appreciate. Wherever he sits with his legs up or his lap flat, I am compelled — I am absolutely driven — to jump up and sit on him. That's where I'm happiest now. It's the centre of the world.

"Albert was saying that we treat Fester like a child substitute," Paul calls out to Jeremy. "That's what he was saying. He says it's classic gay couple stuff. We've settled in the suburbs and we're looking for a child substitute. We haven't procreated or adopted or anything. We've got nothing else to feel responsible for. And so we have latched on to Fester. And he says we fuss over him to excess. That's how it looks to Albert's eyes."

Ungow? I ask. Excess?

WORKING

Now it's time to sit at Paul's desk.

His window is level with the top of his desk. The desk is a flat wooden table, with room for his laptop, a mugful of pens, and a small basket of notebooks. And there's room enough for me to sit on. There are three basic desk positions for Fester Cat. First there's right in front of the laptop. I sit between Paul and his keyboard, pushing my face into his. I nudge him for attention. Somehow he snakes his arms around me and carries on typing, even as I'm kissing him. The warmth of the machine is wonderful.

Then there's the more nonchalant positioning, on the right of the laptop. From here I can keep an eye on Paul, and lean over now and then to scratch my chin on the very corner of his computer screen. Sometimes I do this so well I leave some slobber on the glass, but he doesn't mind.

Then — in some ways, best of all — I sit right in front of the window, with the whole of Chestnut Avenue spread before me. I have a magnificent view of the road in front of us and how it splits into two dead ends. Lots of traffic comes past here. Lots of kids in hoodies, school kids, mums with pushchairs, dodgy-looking blokes, and neighbours that I can recognise. Also, lots of cats. I watch them tracking about, hopping over walls, under gates, and brazenly down the middle of the road. Lots and lots of cats, not all of whom I recognise. And dogs and sometimes, late at night, foxes. I sit up, alert, riveted by the drama outside. To me it's like he telly is to the boys, and I think they understand that.

Paul types away furiously for minutes and hours at a time. Then he stops abruptly. Then he does a bit more. Then he picks out a notebook and goes flipping through quickly, looking for something. Then he starts scribbling madly for page after page and then crossing things out. He uses pens that squeak against the page like baby mice. I can't help myself hopping over and pushing my cold nose against his hand. If I really want his attention I go and sit on the pages of his notebook. If I think he's been working too long and too hard and his attention is starting to fray, I go to interrupt him and I know it's the right thing to do.

We're working together. These are the ways I help him.

As winter comes on and he spends more time up here, in this little room at the front of the house, I'm realising what it is that he does. He writes books.

And it turns out that these books he spends all his time with — reading till late at night, scribbling in the early morning — they're not that mysterious after all. They're not something completely weird and alien. I understand now that I'll never be able to read them, of course not. But I understand that all the marks and squiggles an scribbles, they are just words.

Books are just filled with talk. That's all it is. And that's something I understand. Cat talk, human talk. It's stuff I'm quite used to. So I'm quite happy to watch him sitting here, doing what he has to do.

He talks to me at odd moments through the day. He takes it very seriously, knowing we're having a proper conversation. Knowing I'm taking it all in. He tries out ideas on me.

"Spoiling you! Huh!" he says.

"Ungow," I tell him. Surely it's after twelve by now. Surely it's almost time for lunch?

"You're my first-ever cat, Fester," he tells me. "I've always wanted one. I always suspected that I might be a cat kind of person. But when I was a kid, Mam wouldn't have one. She thought they were stinky, nasty things."

"Ungow!"

"I know! And then, of course, as a student it was always about moving house each year and you couldn't really have pets. Then it was about moving from city to city. And then me and Jeremy were living in different cities . . ."

I like it when he tells me bits about their lives before I came along. I'm slowly building up a picture of who they both are. Paul uses far more words than Jeremy does, of course. He hardly ever shuts up. Only when he's working or reading — and even then, it's words, words, words passing through his mind.

"Really, I don't even know the right way to carry on with a cat. I don't know the right way to be."

"Ungow." I try telling him it's fine. He doesn't have to be any particular way. Just keep on doing his normal stuff. Cats don't need entertaining or babysitting. If I wasn't interested I'd be nowhere near you. I'd zip off somewhere and get on with something else. You're okay. You sit quite still and you do some interesting stuff.

I especially like it when he goes off in one of his daydreams, between bouts of his tap-tapping at the keyboard. He stares into space out of the window just like a cat would. We sit there side by side, staring into the road, into other people's windows, and into the sky.

He says, "Is it the same in the cat world, Fester? Because in the human world there's always someone who thinks they know best. There's someone like Albert who's done a course or read an article and now that makes them the expert. And they know more about the right way to go on than you do. They're only too happy to let you know what it is that you've got wrong."

"Ungow!" Yes, I think, bloomin' Bessy is like that. She of the bad attitude and the biggest bollocks in the world. Somewhere missing in action, under the railway lines with the rough cats from Brunswick Road.

"I've never really had anyone to look after," Paul says. "Well, outside of family stuff. And grown-ups. I mean, I've spent my whole life feeling responsible, and being responsible. But I've never had anyone to look after. No one who depended on me . . ."

Well, I think, standing up and going to the window and taking a deep breath of the breeze that comes whistling in. I've never had anyone to look after, either. I was a pet, then I was a stray. Then I was a pet and a stray again. Now I'm here and I feel more like a member of the household than anything else. Is that daft? I feel like an equal. A colleague. Properly one of the family.

"Hey, Fester," he says, and he pushes the laptop round to show me.

Is he going to show me what he's been writing? He surely doesn't expect me to be able to read?

But the screen has turned into a kind of mirror.

I go to sit beside him and we stare out of the window, both wearing identical expressions. Looking hopefully into the skies above Chestnut Avenue. Maybe starting to feel a bit Christmassy, even. Both of us looking pleased to be sitting at home together.

The whole screen goes FLAAASSSSHH and it turns out it's like a camera. It takes pictures you can keep.

This is the first of many, many pictures we get taken together, sitting there at his desk. It becomes a habit. Many days begin with having our photo taken together. We're both staring out of all these pictures, looking like we're wondering about what's coming next.

DECORATIONS

They drive to a garden centre near Cheadle and they're away for ages that afternoon. There's an excitement about them. They're up to something. I'm not sure what it is.

I sit in the armchair in Paul's study, curled up and glad I'm not out in all that frost.

When they return they've got a tree.

They open the front door and I dash downstairs, sitting on the front doorstep and watching with amusement as they wrestle with this thing. What is this? You've brought a dead tree home? It's a huge, bushy thing, bristling with needles and reeking like somewhere I've never been. Somewhere abroad, maybe. Where there's a whole forest of these things.

They drag it in, laughing and knocking things over, shedding green bits everywhere. I follow cautiously down the hallway, wondering just where they're going to put it. Not the corner of the living room that holds my basket, I hope.

There, by the window. They've already moved a cabinet and there's a space. The great tall thing is too high for the ceiling.

They manoeuvre it into a metal stand they have bought to go with it and we all step back to admire their purchase.

I guess this is some kind of ritual for them. It's the first thing in their Christmas calendar. Boxes come down from the attic. Vast things, six of them, each containing a huge number of ornaments wrapped in tissue paper. Great long twists of paper chains and streamers and these fascinating, metallic festoons of tinsel. I must examine each of these things as they are carefully unloaded.

It all smells very interesting. Again, that blend of aromas from different houses, different times. The houses and Christmases that the boys have shared together elsewhere, each year buying some new tacky decorations to add to the supply. But there are also decorations here going way back in the past. Jeremy's parents have given him a bunch of things that used to go on their tree when he was a kid. There are some ancient homemade snowmen here, made from yellowing cotton-wool balls, and robins cut from painted sugar paper. Nothing from Paul's childhood, though, I notice. He says that a lot of his stuff was thrown out and lost over many house moves. I can sense that he wishes he had this history of stuff, same as Jeremy has.

He tells a story about the first Christmas he and Jeremy had together. It was back in 1996. (Hey, I was alive then. I was a kitten, but I was a long way away, and a long way from knowing them.)

They were in Jeremy's flat, when he was a warden on the university campus in Edinburgh underneath a stretch of mountainous peaks called Arthur's Seat. The two of them weren't going to be together for Christmas itself, they were separating to spend time with their respective parents — Jeremy in Perth, Paul in County Durham. This was their last day together and Paul woke up with a terrible crick in his neck. He sat bolt upright in bed, and felt something tear. The pain was so bad he threw a fit, Jeremy said, and mimed the awful thrashing about and foaming from the mouth Paul did. Jeremy was scared to death. Ten years after he could laugh about it, but back then it was terrible.

"I couldn't move for about twenty-four hours," Paul explains. "I was completely seized up. I had to wear about thirty scarves to keep my head on. And that was the morning that my father — who I hadn't seen in maybe ten years — phoned up! He had got Jeremy's phone number from my mam, and he phoned up to say that my Little Nanna had died. It was horrible. I sat there and I could barely move and here was this virtual stranger sobbing down the phone. And then he started shrieking and screaming at me because I told him there was no way I was going to the funeral. He said that I was heartless and horrible and he had lost his mother and how did I think he felt? And then he started screaming that I was a queer and that I hadn't grown up right. Without his influence in my life I had grown up wrong and perverted."

I stare at both Paul and Jeremy as we sit amongst all the Christmas decorations. Jeremy shrugs. "Most of his family stories are like this," he tells me.

Paul goes on, "Anyway, after that, I lay back down, just about blacking out with the pain of this neck thing. Jeremy tried to make me go to the emergency room for a neck brace or an X-ray or something, but there was just no way. I was in my dressing gown and pants and I was upset about my Little Nanna, as it happened. She was the one who sang Shirley Bassey songs in working men's clubs round the northeast in the 1970s. I had been very fond of her, but sh wouldn't see me after I said I didn't want to see my awful father anymore. Anyhow, I lay down and Jeremy goes off to put a soothing record on to calm me down."

Wow! I think. Families! Maybe I'm glad I never had one. Cat families can be pretty fierce, though maybe not as bad as humans. Humans can really torture each other. Cats only do bad stuff in each other's presence. They can't ring each other up or send nasty letters or e-mails.

Sitting under the Christmas tree that morning, I was hearing my first horror story from Paul about the past.

Jeremy is fetching out vinyl Christmas records, just like he did in the story. That's one of the things about Jeremy. He still has all his records, and likes to put them on an old turntable. He loves the crackle and hiss and pops when the needle goes down. I love that too. It's a noise that makes me shiver. When he puts his records on I go to lie directly between the huge dark speakers with the fabric front that, when no one's watching, I like to click a little with my claws. The hiss and crackles on the grooves feel wonderful when you put sensitive cat ears close to the sound.

Paul says, "The record he put on was one had known as a kid. It was one that my

Little Nanna had bought me when I was a toddler. By some huge, amazing coincidence Jeremy had chosen the one record that we had played every Christmas Eve right through my childhood. The single record that felt the most Christmassy to me. One that Mam had flung out into the bin, along with all my other records, when I was away at college, so I hadn't heard it in quite a few years."

"Ungow?" I ask, keen to know what this record was.

"I'd had the same record all my life too," Jeremy explains. Then he shows me the cover, and goes over to put the needle on the record.

Pinky and Perky's Christmas Album?

It's a record made by singing pigs?

The first song comes on and it's two falsetto pigs shouting at each other and then singing "Santa Claus Is Coming to Town." It's possibly the most hideous thing I have ever heard. But these two dafties are gazing at each other like it's the most moving thing on earth.

In these couple of weeks leading to my first Christmas in their house, I get to hear all of their collected Christmas songs. And I hear a lot of their Christmas stories too. I get the feeling that they have told each othe these tales, again and again, over the ten years they've had together. They're pleased I'm here to listen for the first time, making it all new again for them.

Okay, I tell them. Enough singing pigs and stories. Food now.

THEIR STORY

I like to hear the tales of when they were first together. They are my human beings and I have adopted them. I want to share their whole story.

They are gay men, Bessy said, with that almost disapproving look on her face.

We gave her a row about that, and that was the first time Korky and I really stood up against Bessy. Though I didn't quite know what she meant by the gay men thing. I guess I do now. I still don't see anything wrong or unusual about it. They're just Paul and Jeremy, and they're together. I can't imagine them any other way. They've been together for as long as I've been alive, closest we've been able to work out the sums.

They're my humans. I put them to bed at night. I walk over them and their duvet and sit first on one, staring into his face, and then the other. This is one of the tasks I have in this house of theirs. I make sure they are settled down for the night. And when they are, I go to lie on the landing, at the top of the twisty staircase, to look out for monsters.

I keep a discreet distance and stay on that landing, in case they get up to any of that sexy stuff.

When they're finished having a cuddle and stuff, I go back to the bed, squoosh Paul aside, and get comfy on the blue satin blanky.

Jeremy sleeps deeply through every night, snoring thunderously.

Paul's an insomniac. He can't help his mind ticking over.

Sometimes in the night he tells me stories.

He told me how the two of them first met.

There's this grand, wonderful city in the north, in Scotland, called Edinburgh. Paul moved there after college, and he had a whole bunch of friends there. He stayed for a couple of years, through his midtwenties, when it was time to figure out where his life was going.

It's quite good, learning that human lives go in phases like cat lives. They move to new places, have a look around, and wonder if they can stick it out. Sniffing the air and scratching in the dirt. Not so different.

He lived at first in a tiny, freezing flat in

the very middle of the city. The only way in and out was up the metal gantries of a fire escape. While he was there he was preparing to bring out his first book, and these were exciting times. He went out each day with his notebooks and sat in different cafés in the Old Town and the New Town and wrote like a demon. Just anything and everything that came into his head, filling thousands of pages. Having sold his first novel, he was teaching himself, all over again, how to write.

Oh, we're quite blasé about writing novels and stuff round this house. It's just what we do. I've had it all explained to me and I'm quite familiar with the process. It's about going a long way in your mind while sitting very still. Again, very catlike, and I approve.

Paul was also looking for the love of his life.

His flatmate would tell him, "I don't think you're going to find him in the places you're looking."

He shrugged. He didn't know where the love of his life would be, and neither did his flatmate. Nobody knew how these things would work out. It was all random. That's what life is like. You just have to make sure you put yourself out there. You have to put yourself into the path of the speeding, random atoms and elements and stuff. Otherwise you'll never know who or what you might have missed.

Lots of exciting bits, lots of false hopes and disappointments. All that midtwenties crap. Everyone acting crazily for a little while. He remembered Christmas Eve 1995 particularly well, he tells me. When Princes Street and George Street — two long and usually very busy roads — were sheeted over with ice at midnight. And he and his friends returned from the pub, having had nachos and margaritas and the only record playing on the jukebox had been "Wonderwall" by Oasis. They slid and skidded on the ice, all the way through the empty city centre, all the way home.

Many nights he would slip out for a drink at CC Blooms, which was a nightclub and bar at the top of Leith Walk, across the way from the big Catholic church. It was the cheapest and tackiest gay bar in town and he loved it, especially karaoke night and "Step Back in Time" night, in the tiny basement disco. He would stay out till five in the morning when it was "Step Back in Time" and they played endless disco songs.

The place was full of disco bunnies, though. Already at twenty-five he was feeling too old for messing about with anyone daft.

Just when he was at the point of giving in, and agreeing with his flatmate that he'd never meet anyone decent in such a dive — he bumped into Jeremy.

It was one night after a terrible breakup with someone he'd been seeing. Not a no-hoper, not a drongo — but someone with whom there was no possible future. He was at the pictures with a mate, and, having split off and said good-bye, Paul decided on a whim to have a last drink at CC Blooms. In that cavernous, dry-icy place that smelled of spilled lager, mingled aftershaves, poppers, and sweat.

He met Duncan, who was a bloke he'd had coffee with a couple of times. A slightly foppish, aloof bloke who played piano. He had a look of someone from a Merchant Ivory film. Duncan chatted in his desultory way (he always seemed as if he was longing to be somewhere else) and he said he was moving to Berlin, and taking his piano with him, which was going to cost a fortune. Then he noticed that someone in a bright white shirt was emerging from the gloom near the bar and coming over.

"I'll introduce you to Jeremy," Duncan said.

And Paul turned round.

He was tall, broad, and blond, with a little quiff at the top of his slightly pointed head. He wore pale blue jeans, a crisp white shirt, and trendy, tiny glasses. His shoes were orange snakeskin. And he smiled at them both.

"I don't know how the dog thing started." Paul laughs. "But it started right there. This idea that Jeremy was a dog. Madly fond, and tail-waggy and panting all over me. Like a dog with hands. That's how he was that night. He came bounding out of the foggy shadows of that tacky bar and we looked at each other and that was it."

I stare at him. "What? You thought Jeremy was a dog?"

"Well, he *was* a bit. Quite a lot. Like a big golden retriever or something. When I told him, later on that night, that that's how he seemed, he played up to it. It became this big joke. He would pant and lick my face and jump all over me. After a few days he said, 'What am I doing? I don't do all this doggy stuff. I've never done anything like this in my life. What am I turning into? YOU'VE done this to me!' "

"Sounds weird." I frown, licking my paws. Humans pretending to be animals. Huh.

He tells me how they started talking, sitting on these metal bar stools. Next thing they knew, Duncan had sort of melted away. He had vanished. Under all the disco noise they hadn't even noticed him saying good-bye. Through the main door, past the bouncers, they could see him unchaining his bike, hopping onto it, and wheeling away. He had left them to it — whether crossly, or whether quietly and nicely, they never knew. They never saw him again.

"He was like a slightly snooty good fairy," says Paul. "He introduced us and then his work was done. I imagine him sitting in Berlin, banging away on his baby grand piano . . . and he's there still, with his floppy hair and his insular expression . . ."

Paul and Jeremy talked and found, after about twenty minutes, that they were holding hands.

"Oh, really," I say, and make a noise like I'm coughing up a really sicky hairball.

"No, it's true! We didn't realise we were even doing it. I remember him telling me about growing up in Perth, and what he was doing now, being a warden at the campus and all, and I remember looking at this lovely pink expanse of collarbone that was showing under the open neck of his shirt. And my hands were so warm in his. It was like we had made a date to do this without ever knowing it."

I roll my eyes. "So did you go back to his? Did you do the dirty deed straightaway and have a special cuddle?"

"Of course!" He laughs. "But we went to mine, not his, because it was closest. Just a few steps away, really. I don't even remember any discussion about it. But what I do remember is, halfway up the steps to my front door, Jeremy asked me what my second name was. And I told him and he paused a moment on the staircase and said, 'Oh!' He looked pretty surprised. Then he said, 'I bought your first novel! I bought it just today in Waterstones.' "

"Get away," I tell him. "He was having you on."

Paul shakes his head. "No, it was true. I saw it the next day when I went round his flat. He had all sorts of wonderful fiction in hardback — Italo Calvino, Alasdair Gray, Günter Grass . . . and me! There I was."

"Well, that must have freaked you out," I tell him. "It would have me. If cats lived in flats. If they wrote novels. If they were complete sluts."

"It didn't freak me out," Paul said. "It just made me feel . . . reassured, if anything. I always feel reassured by coincidences and weird mischance stuff."

"Do you?" I frown. "Are you saying you're religious and everything is down to divine interference?"

He shakes his head. "No, not that. I don't know what. I think it's all random. I do. But I think that . . . sometimes . . . if you're ready for it, and you're listening hard . . . it's like something in the galaxy rhymes. Things chime off each other and it's just right. Does that make sense?"

I narrow my eyes at him. He thinks I'm dozing off. But I'm not. This is my appraising look. One of a whole range of appraising looks I have perfected.

I wink at him, very slowly.

Ungow!

He's hit upon something most cats believe in absolutely. The galaxy rhymes. You just have to sit nicely and patiently and listen for it happening. You can't coax or force it. You just have to wait.

"Mind," Paul adds. "After we'd had a cup of tea in the kitchen and then raced each other into bed, he did tell me that he'd found my book in the bargain bin. Only six flaming months after it was published! Reduced to a bloody pound or something!"

"I imagine the cuddle and stuff came as some consolation," I tell him. "Ungow!"

It seems strange to think of them climbing into bed together back then in the mid-1990s, and there not being a Fester Cat there to organise them.

But everything they did prior to 2006 I have decided to regard as rehearsal. They were just trying to get everything together, ready for 2006 and their life here, with me and forever now. Ungow!

HAMPER

Right before Christmas the hamper arrives.

We've already had the post that morning, and I've sat on the doorstep watching as Paul signed the postman's electronic pad. Now we're answering the door again and it's a man with a van from Marks & Spencer. They've brought a cardboard box the size of a house.

Why is it I love cardboard boxes like I do? I love the sound of fingers and claws scratching against those hollow sides. I love the feel of corrugated cardboard against my jaw and chops.

Also, I love the Styrofoam packing material. When Paul unloads the mysterious gift and Jeremy comes down from his study to help, there's a lot of these floating white question-mark things that need chasing and pouncing on. I'm afraid I start acting a bit giddy. I catch myself skipping like Korky would. It's really not dignified for a cat of my vintage.

Inside the box: a picnic hamper made of wickerwork. A lid tied down with straps. Intriguing smells wafting through the twiggy lattice. The whole thing is creaking and aching for me to sharpen my claws on.

I flex a tentative paw and extend my talons . . .

"Don't scratch it, Fester! We haven't even got it open yet!"

It's a hamper filled with Christmas stuff. Coffee and wine and biscuits and fancy tea, and stuff that humans would care about. Everything crackles deliciously in cellophane. But there's also stuff that's packed in ice. Stuff that has my nose going crazy and pulsating when they open it up. Great hunks of slippery salmon. A platter of smoked gammon.

I start shouting. They've heard me saw "mow" quite a lot, in my politely questioning mode. They've heard me say "Ungow" an awful lot, as it's the nearest thing I have to human language. But they've not heard me throw my head back, open up my throat, and yodel. Not yet. But this is something I find I can do now. It's me at full blast. Forget the cute tinkling and jingling that I do with the Christmas bells they've attached to my collar (my new collar!). Yeah, forget

all that. That's cute and sweet and sometimes I'm in the mood for that.

Sometimes what you really need to get
your point across is a bloomin' good shout.

It works. It's too early for Christmas, but
they exchange a glance and come to a decision. Smoked salmon for lunch. Thin brown
bread with butter, black pepper, and lemon
wedges, but I don't care about all that. Just
give me the good stuff, boys, those near-
transparent slivers. Those cat-sized steaks
all mangled up. Meltingly perfect for a cat
with very few choppers.

Shouting

The hamper was sent by Jeremy's parents, who I'm about to meet.

They're travelling by train, because it's too long a drive from Perth to Manchester. I understand his parents — Peter and Rita — are of advanced years. They're staying in a hotel in town, and coming here to our house to be fed and to pay a visit.

They haven't been before. Both boys fuss over whether the house is "nice" enough. Well, Paul more than Jeremy. Jeremy fusses less on the whole about everything. He's much more laid-back. Much more take-us-as-you-find-us. Paul can get himself wound up into a tizzy and this can cause rows between them.

When they argue I watch for a while, and trot back and forth between them, going: "Look! It's me! Pay attention to me! Stop being awful to each other! And just be glad you've got Fester for a go-between! Go on

— tell me — tell me what to say to the other one. You still love him, don't you? You don't really care about the mess in the hall or the dusty shelves? All of that isn't really important, is it? It isn't a test, it's a visit! C'mon. Make up! Stop sniping! Stop being so silly and nervy and dissatisfied!"

It comes out in the form of a lot of padding about — up and down the stairs when they go to opposite ends of the house. It takes the form of a lot of gentle "Ungows!" and nudging of shins and a lot of tinkling of these effete Christmas bells.

My emergency standby is getting right in front of one of them, and then the other one, and going FLLLOOOMMMMP! I fling myself on the floor at their feet. Demanding attention and a tummy tickle. When I've got their attention in this way, then I can say, "All right! Make up! Stop fighting! Everything will be fine! It's just a visit! Don't lose your heads, you dafties!"

I sit on the kitchen table and watch Paul cooking.

He's going overboard, of course. Trying to prove something, I shouldn't wonder. Don't know what. Maybe just that he can be a good host. They've never come to visit here before, he tells me. This is the first time his in-laws are going to see this home.

He makes some kind of sticky lamb, Moroccan style. He uses dates and pomegranates and all kinds of fruity muck. Ruining perfectly good meat. Meat that smelled so heavenly when it was pink and raw, and then even better when he was turning wodges of it over to brown in the hot pan. Luckily, he set a little aside for me. Only after I demonstrated some more shouting.

When I shout I go: "Arrrruuuuu-arrraaaaaaaaaauuuuuuulll!"

Which is handy when the person you're shouting at is called Paul.

A bit of practicing and it's not long before I've adapted my natural heartfelt cry. I try it out on him when I'm sitting on that table and he's flustered, going about with pans and pots and whisking egg whites to stiff pointy peaks for a *tarte au citron* he's rashly decided to make.

I go: "Paaaaaaaa-arrrruuuuuu-arrrr-aaaaaaaauuuuuuulllll!"

And he almost drops all of his utensils.

It's a bit of a yodel, but it's clearly, unmistakably the sound of his little cat shouting his name at him.

Paul stares at me.

I sit a little more smartly on the very corner of the kitchen table, straightening my shoulders and pressing my paws together. I'm sitting to cat attention, as he calls it. Puffing out my chest and just — quite subtly — smirking.

Then there's a clatter at the front door and Jeremy is showing his parents into the hallway. They've arrived.

THE VISIT

This pair don't seem to mind that they've got a cat sitting at one of the chairs round the table. As we eat and talk Jeremy puts old records on the player, and I study his parents. They're tired from their long journey, but they paused in their hotel to dress up for this evening. His father's got soft white hair and he wears a tweed jacket and a tie. His mother's in a silk blouse. The two of them gaze around our colourful house, nodding and smiling as the boys feed them, and they all talk about stuff.

I'm picking out bits of pomegranate seed and funny stuff from the lamb I've been given.

Jeremy tells the story-so-far of Fester Cat to his parents, and they seem suitably impressed. They marvel over my glossy coat and they laugh at my curled lip, and the way I stare at them each in turn, as if I'm really listening.

After dinner the boys take away all the dinner plates and dishes, and out come the silly old board games. KerPlunk, Buckaroo, Operation. These are things that everyone remembers from years ago, apparently. They involve lots of intricate parts, and much messing about. Buzzers go off unexpectedly, plastic parts are propelled suddenly through the air, and everything collapses in a noisy rush. Though Jeremy suspects his parents would rather be playing bridge or backgammon, soon everyone's having a laugh. At one point, I'm so excited by it all, I'm up on that table and batting at the KerPlunk tower with my paws, trying to make all the marbles and cocktail sticks fall down.

Later, when they sit on the settees and have coffee, I'm looking at each lap in turn, wondering who I should go to. They aren't really cat people, I don't think. They seem a bit wary of me as I patrol the living room and hop onto the arm of each chair in turn.

Rita is telling the tale of adopting her sons. They were one year apart, and Jeremy was the second. Near the end of the 1960s, this was; a very long time ago. They were shown to a room of glass cribs and told to examine each baby. Jeremy was the last one they saw. "He was just like a bundle of twigs," Rita tells Paul. "And we decided that he had to be the one. We wanted to take him home that very minute and feed him up, so that's what we did."

Now everyone's looking at Jeremy, who seems very pleased with himself at the idea of being chosen. Everything worked out for the best, I think, and I hop onto Peter's lap. He's surprised for a moment, and then pleased. "There, there, old chap," he tells me.

I'm fascinated really, hearing about human arrangements and families and stuff.

And by now I feel terrifically festive.

CHRISTMAS WORMS

Just before Christmas comes, guess what?

I've got worms.

I am mortified.

This is the day after Jeremy's parents have returned home to Scotland after their few days here. Everyone is worn out with running around.

It's evening and we're settling in for the night with a film on the TV. I'm standing on Jeremy as he lies down on the settee. Just as I'm padding round in a circle, changing my position, he cries out in surprise.

"There's something sticking out of his bum! And it's . . . waving at me!"

Honestly, I feel like running away and hiding.

Both fellas fly into a panic. They start to make me feel more than embarrassed. They get me worried too. What is it that's wrong with me? What have they seen? Maybe it's something terrible and fatal and I'm not even going to make it through till Christmas Day?

Which would be just dreadful. For I have seen the turkey that they have bought. It fills almost half the fridge. They had to take out a shelf to fit it in. I have named this turkey George and sometimes I sit by the fridge, waiting for him to come out to play.

But what is this thing that's scared Jeremy so badly?

I try to slink away, under a cupboard, to have a look.

Paul phones Jasmine, his friend from the university. She's a writer like him, apparently, and a keen cat lover. They talk for some time. And he comes back saying, "It's worms. It's okay. Quite common. He just needs some tablets and stuff."

Quite common!

"Jasmine says they pick these things up quite naturally, from being outside and eating all sorts of stuff. It just needs sorting quickly, because it won't be doing him any good."

Well, I'm still mortified. Worms! Worms at Christmas. Not very bloomin' festive, is it?

I go to flomp down miserably in my basket while Jeremy goes out to the vet's. Now I daren't even look at my bum in case I see something staring back at me.

How come, when I was a stray, stuff like this never bothered me? I never even noticed things like this.

But back then I was starving all the time, wasn't I? And every scabby inch of me scratched like crazy. I think I'm just getting used to a certain level of comfort. I'm suburban and bourgeois — just like Bessy said!

I lie there reflecting that I hate the thought of that Jasmine knowing all about my worms and what's up my bum. The fact that she could show off her cat knowledge on my account and know what was wrong without even looking at me. I have to admit that she is another of the boys' friends that I'm not sure about.

Don't get me wrong. There are plenty of their friends who I've met, who I like. I really do. I like Deborah, who's a librarian. She's one of the few women whose laps I will sit on. She's very careful and sweet and doesn't make a fuss. I like to go to people who don't make a right show of how pleased they are to have me sitting with them. I also like Karen and Mark, who've moved in a few doors down from us. We've seen them once or twice, and they seem fine too. Cat people.

Well, Jasmine is a cat person, but I'm not

so keen on her.

She comes dashing in, like she's always in a rush. She wears all these shawls and scarves and things like a big bundle of bedding, with uncomfortable-looking jewels hanging off her ears and round her neck. She calls everyone darling, including me, as if she can't be arsed remembering anyone's name. And she makes a big production number out of knowing the answer to everything. "Oh, darling, don't you know? How funny. It's really quite simple and straightforward, you know. Your poor little moggy has got worms! All of his insides are filled with horrid, wriggling parasites! That's why he's looking so sorry for himself!"

She pops round to visit, and amid all the boring talk of her latest novel and stuff about her publisher, she spouts off like this about my intestinal parasites. If I had more than two teeth I would bite her. The silly woman even tries to pick me up as if she's a vet. I wriggle like crazy.

"Oh, these animals." She sighs dramatically. "We let them into our lives, don't we? And they go through all their little dramas. Sometimes they have dramas as big and as traumatic as humans do. And then, eventually, they break our hearts. And it happens again and again. And we let it happen. We let it happen again and again. Because in the end they are worth it. It's worth having this little scrap of company and animal comfort in our lives."

Then she puts me back down in my basket. Yeah, thanks a lot, love. Nice speech.

Jeremy brings the tablets and they taste bloomin' awful. I can spit pretty well. Pthfoot. Pthffft. He retrieves the pills and Jasmine watches, amused, as they struggle to feed me the things. She makes me feel self-conscious.

I wonder vaguely what her novels are about. Probably something awful. I bet they're all nosy and self-important and looking down on people. They'll be all about people she feels sorry for. Ugh.

Paul hits on the idea of coating the tablets in chicken liver pâté.

Not bad!

CREATURES OF HABIT

All these Christmases turn into one.

Cats like routines. That's what their friend Jasmine says, and she's the expert on everything. She says that cats like the consoling nature of things happening regularly, just the same each time.

"Like you do, Paul," she says, necking the pink champagne. "You're all creatures of habit."

"Hmm," he says — amazed by her insight.

Jeremy and I exchange a glance at this. I think we're both highly sceptical about Jasmine. Paul is so easily taken in by people. He's really no judge of character at all. He's lucky he's got Jeremy and me to keep him right.

But as for habits and routines, it seems that I love them anyhow. And I love how that first Christmas and all the ones we share afterwards work out pretty much in the same pattern.

There are visits to and from neighbours on Christmas Eve. I sit by the living room window, watching for dusk and Cat Passeggiata. This happens only on certain evenings in the year, when all the local cats make a circuit of everyone's back garden along Chestnut Avenue. It's a very stately, elegant progress. Everyone looking out for everyone else, and greeting each other solemnly. Tonight I can't really be faffed, though. I don't ask to be let outside for a gadabout. I'm content to watch from here, where the fire is crackling away.

My gang's all gone. There's no Bessy and no Korky for me to "passeggiata" about with. However, I do see Whisper having a sniff round our patio, and Three-Legged Freddie goes galumphing by, looping the loop. Whisper sprays our sun lounger as if to cock a snook at us.

I even see Granddad Smokey. He's hauling himself heavily over the garden walls and staring beadily at all the local cats as he meets them.

The new neighbours' cats make a trip across three gardens and an alleyway to sit in our back. They are both tortoiseshells — one grey, one marmalade. Scoobie and Rowan. They jump up on our window ledge in order to call their owners home for

Christmas Eve. All the humans are astonished by these cat-calls.

Our visitors leave and I'm alone with Paul and Jeremy. *The Nutcracker Suite* comes on through those rumbling, wonderful speakers on the wooden floor.

Jeremy claims never to have lists of favourite things and he despairs when Paul asks him . . . Ten favourite musicals? Ten favourite sitcoms? But when Jeremy was in junior school the teacher asked his class to name their favourite record. Jeremy's hand went up.

"Can I have all three records in the CBS Masterworks boxed set of Tchaikovsky's *Nutcracker Suite* as played by the Toronto Symphony, Andrew Davies conducting?"

He had saved up for it over a number of weeks, and can still remember bringing it home in a brown paper bag. He took the vinyl records out of their sleeves and dusted them. He put them on the player, one side after the next. The copy we're listening to tonight is the same one, all these years later.

I think his teacher probably thought he was a smartarse. This was the same teacher who, when listening to their class reading out their "What I did at the weekend" essays gave Jeremy a hard time. Jeremy had said his mother cooked chili con carne.

"Don't be ridiculous!" the teacher shouted. "There's no such thing!"

"But there is! My mother quite often cooks chili con carne!"

He was sent out for being rude. His face was red with suppressed fury. He was ostracised for claiming the existence of dubious Mexican dishes.

Jeremy is forever railing against authority figures. I am coming to realise this. He gets especially cross when those with authority are morons, as he puts it. Jeremy spends a lot of his time being exasperated.

For their tea the boys have tomato soup, because for Paul it's the essence of Christmas Eve. He says his family always had tomato soup then — something light before the excesses of Christmas started.

They've got the radio playing old hits in the kitchen and Al Stewart's "Year of the Cat" comes on. It's only been on a few moments when I come tearing into the room. They fall about laughing because, apparently, from where they're sitting, sipping their soup, it looked very much like I'd heard the song and came dashing in, ready to dance to it. As if "Year of the Cat" was my favourite bloomin' song of all time o' something. But it wasn't that! It real' wasn't! I smelled the melting butter on their toast! As if I'd dance to a soppy song like that! Just because it's about a cat or something. And now I feel a bit foolish, actually.

"Never mind, Fester Cat," says Paul, and he goes to open a special pouch of cat food for me. Whiskas pouches! Turkey flavour. Very festive. And I tuck in very enthusiastically at my feeding station by the fridge.

As it happens, my two favourite songs for dancing to are disco tunes. They are "Don't Take Away the Music" and "You're My First, My Last, My Everything." If anything makes me want to dance like a daft human, they do.

Christmas Eve gets late and we watch all of their favourite Christmas TV shows from their vast collection of old TV rubbish. They keep all the discs in folders with pages that — you guessed it — are great for clicking claws on. *The Good Life,* Christmas 1977; *The Snowman,* Christmas 1982; *K9 and Company,* Christmas 1981; *Cagney and Lacey,* Christmas 1982; *Crossroads' Christmas,* 1979. It's too much bad TV for Jeremy and he drifts upstairs to mess about on his computer and Paul stretches out on the settee. "Watch this with me, Fester! Jump up! Bounce! Look, it's *The Very Best of Larry*

171

Grayson's Generation Game from Christmas 1979!"

Actually, I'm quite pleased he's a fan of old things. I'm pretty much vintage myself.

Ungow!

But I'm still ever so nimble!

I spring onto the settee and hop onto his chest. I settle heavily, with a deep sigh, lying face-to-face with Paul as he watches his silly old TV show. He's drifting off to sleep. And I am too. I smell the sherry fumes on his breath and the wood smoke from the fire. I bask in all the Christmas-tree lights. And by the time Jeremy comes thumping down the stairs to make a pot of tea, it turns out it's after midnight. It's Christmas already.

Every Christmas Eve goes like this, for us.

Happy Christmas, everyone.

EARLY MORNINGS

We go downstairs together.

Me and Paul do this every single morning, every day the same. It's our routine,
while Jeremy's still sleeping.

Sometimes Paul wakes up first, and he
finds me curled up lying beside him. I come
wake as soon as he sits up, though. I don't

want to miss a single thing.

Other times I'm awake first and he's still fast asleep. This can be very early sometimes and I have to take drastic measures. I stand by the side of his bed and shout. "Mow," first of all. Then, "Ungow." And then a fully fledged, "Paaaaaauuuuaaauuurrraaaau-uuulllllll!"

If that doesn't work and he won't get up, I start in on the scratching. Book spines. I go round all the shelves closest to the ground and begin sharpening my claws. The noise drives him crazy, because he knows what damage I'm doing to his books.

Failing that, I jump on his bedside table and stare at him. Then I jump on his pillow and put my paw in his face. I dab him lightly with it. Just a small prod or two. Checking that he's still alive. And I nudge him with my nose. *Boop.*

Boop. Boop.

Then I hop onto his chest and start shouting again.

He's usually pretty good, and gets up before I have to run through the whole of the above list more than twice.

He gets up and does his best to be bright and sprightly in the morning. I lead him to the bathroom, where he does a wee, and I supervise while he checks out my litter an

174

sorts it out. "You got it all in the litter tray! Very good! Clever Fester! Very tidy!" Or, alternatively: "You didn't get it all in the litter."

He washes and brushes his teeth and I sit there by the door, patiently, sitting at cat attention. I wait until he's finished at the sink, then he turns and pats me on the head before he goes by. I don't know why. This drives me crazy. When his palm comes down I push my whole head upwards to meet it, until he's cupping my whole skull and pushing my ears down. And then I kind of wriggle under his palm. It's heaven.

I trot ahead of him to the top of the stairs and sit there as he pauses on the bend in the staircase. He crouches on the stair and kisses me between my ears. He says I smell biscuity.

Then I'm free to run down the stairs ahead of him, doing what he calls bunny hops, with my back legs pushing in tandem as I leap down step after step. The sight of my flashing white legs hurrying down to breakfast always makes him laugh.

Every morning is the same as this. If any part of our routine is missing, it seems like our morning doesn't quite go right.

Coming down the stairs is one of my favourite bits of the day.

Discovering the downstairs of our house again. Finding everything just as we left it. Walking into the promise of doing all our favourite things, all over again, and having the time and the energy to do them all once more.

He goes round opening curtains, putting on lights, opening windows. I follow him round each bit of the circuit, anticipating what needs doing next. We stop at the front door and he deals with the barrage of bolts and locks. He unhooks the chain and twists the Yale and pulls open the door so that it is open to the front street.

I sit there inhaling that glorious scent of morning in Manchester. It's all fresh blue and damp and hectic with birdsong and the blare of nearby traffic. I sit there inhaling deeply as he picks up the milk bottles and flicks off the slugs.

"Do you want to go out for a run around?" he asks me, ever so polite.

In my earlier days with the boys I might do this. I'd dash out into the terrace and go for a scamper. Sometimes I'd pop into the old woman's garden next door, where the grass grows long and luxurious. Sometimes I just need that little bit of grass, and I chomp it carefully, dutifully. Or, other times, I'd like to have a dash about on the tarmac of the roads and sniff about under some cars.

As time goes on, I feel less like doing all this first thing in the morning, I must admit. All I'm really thinking about is breakfast. And Paul starts to think, over the months and years, that I'm not to be trusted out the front, playing in the traffic. He observes some hairy moments in which I seem too much of a daredevil, dashing out in front of cars. He catches me lying in the bend in the road, where the sun is shining one afternoon. I've flomped completely and I'm rolling around, flicking my ears with my paws, turning belly side up for the sun. Right in the path of any oncoming cars. I don't recall this particular bit of recklessness myself, but I'll take his word for it.

Thing is, when you become a full-time house cat you do end up losing some of your street smarts. It's just one of those unfortunate things. More than made up for in the form of jellyish, gravyish cat food in pouches, but nevertheless. My life is changing, all the same. I am getting used to being looked after.

Ah, well. So what. I'm an older gentleman cat, and I'm glad someone's looking after me.

Then we pad down the hallway to the

kitchen. I sit by my feeding station, which I will have, inevitably, emptied during the night.

Christmas morning is the same as every other day, except for the fact it's brilliantly exciting.

All our routines are the same, except that when we get to the bottom of the stairs I can see at once that Santa Claus has been. I was pretty sceptical about the Santa stuff that the boys were going on about. They hung up fancy stockings on the mantelpiece and I went along with it. But — lo and behold! — when we reach the bottom stair . . . do my eyes deceive me?

There's a baby mouse crouching in the shadow of the coat stand. Paul doesn't notice it and he's about to pass by. I sit there dumbfounded at the bottom of the stairs. Thank you, Santa! Yes! I believe in you! Ungow!

It's definitely a baby mouse. Very dark, panting very hard, hoping to creep behind the jumbled heap of shoes. Its black eyes bulge and glitter at me. It's hoping to back away quietly and to shoot down between the floorboards into that dark and airy cellar. No chance. Happy Christmas. I pounce.

There's a struggle then as Paul realises what I'm doing. His shouting spoils m concentration and I drop the Christmas toy out of my mouth. It shoots across the floor and Paul is the one who manages to catch it, somehow. He's not the most coordinated, so I'm surprised. He's got the mouse holed up inside one of Jeremy's shoes. At first I think he's going to present it to me. Congratulations — and here is your Christmas mouse!

But he simply unlocks the front door and sets it free in the front garden. It goes away with a sort of limping hop. I tell Paul, "That's a waste. It'll die anyway. Some other cat will have it. Or, it'll never get home to its family. You've sent it into the wilderness. It's only a baby mouse. What do you think will become of it? It'll run away to the railway embankment and meet a much worse fate than it would do with me."

Paul stares at me. "You were going to rip him to pieces!"

"Ungow." I march past Paul, towards the kitchen. "Not necessarily. He was my Christmas mouse. I'd have carried him about in my mouth till he was soggy. Then I might have played with him a bit. I don't know. We'd see how we got along. But I wouldn't have put him out on the streets on Christmas morning. I'm not cruel."

In the kitchen he puts on the first of their

Christmas CDs (it takes all day to get through them all) and he opens the fridge to study George the turkey.

Ah, here's my playmate for Christmas. I get to know this turkey very well over the next few days of Christmas, and then again, every Christmas that comes after.

Isn't that just the best Christmas miracle? You begin with this giant pink bird and it becomes an array of delicious meals. You end up eating every single part of it as the days go by. And then, next year, without fail, the turkey is born again, perfect. He comes back from his annual obliteration, and sits in your fridge once more. Sometimes bigger and more delicious than ever.

Paul starts cooking straightaway. He makes tea and puts out cat food. Then he's peeling vegetables and pulling out a little parcel that's wedged inside the giant bird. I know what's in there. I can smell them. Bloody bits of wonderful innards. I sit there agog on the kitchen table, sniffing hard and shouting as he roasts the turkey heart and liver and neck.

Somehow, later on, the roasted heart ends up on the kitchen floor. I think it's when I'm up on the cooker, having a mooch, while he's upstairs, telling Jeremy to get up. There's a hot, cooked heart rolling about on the floor and I'm pouncing on it, batting at it, chasing it round chair legs.

I'm hoping that turkey heart hockey becomes another of our holiday traditions.

OLD CHRISTMASES

Going downstairs was a big part of Christmases for Paul when he was a kid.

His mam would lead the way — silently, carefully — at an impossible hour in the morning, when the house was still dark. His whole body was jumping about inside with excitement. He'd half close his eyes going downstairs, knowing what the routine was; once he was outside their living room, his mam would go inside first, to check that Santa had been. He knew that she was just as excited as he was.

Then he would put both hands over his eyes and walk into the room. Only when he was standing in the middle could he take his hands away and look around.

But even before he did that he could smell the changes. There was always the smell of fresh fruit. Tangerines and shiny red apples. Mingling with the smell of artificial spray snow on the tree and windows.

He'd open his eyes and it would be brilliant with colour in there. His mam always went crazy on Christmas presents. There were heaps everywhere, wrapped in bright paper.

Before any presents could be opened the Pinky and Perky album would go on the turntable. Mugs of tea would appear.

One of his best memories of this, he was given a sled with blue metal runners. Such a boyish present. Such an outdoorsy present. Not like Paul at all, really. But he loved it at first sight. He couldn't believe it. Sitting there in the middle of the front room. Perfect for the hills by their housing development and by the junior school. Snow had fallen that year, and already the hills were glassy-sided with kids skidding down on plastic bags and sleds. But nothing like this. This came from Hardings, the posh toy shop in town.

There were other gifts. He remembers a *Doctor Who* jigsaw that year, with Tom Baker — it was 1977. And books, of course. The Disney annual. His mam said, "I'm sorry there aren't as many presents as last year," and he couldn't believe she was saying it. But surely there were more? And what did he care about that, anyway? There was all *this*. He looked at her and couldn't make her understand. He didn't have the words for it. These were the most brilliant presents. These were perfect.

His dad came to pick him up too early. He was meant to come at lunchtime. He turned up at 7:30 a.m. Paul was going to his Little Nanna's to be with his dad's family for the rest of the day, and Mam would be alone.

"Why are you so early?" he heard his mam hissing in the kitchen.

"This is what we agreed," his dad insisted. "So, did you get me a present, then?"

"Are you kidding?"

His dad was one of those people whose skin was so thick he just didn't understand anything. Paul already understood that. Their living room had hardly any furniture because his dad had taken it when he moved out. And he was standing in the kitchen asking the wife he'd split up from for presents.

Paul's life for a few years was going back and forth between them, though his home was with his mam. At weekends he'd be at his dad's, who wanted him playing football and other stuff like that. His dad would fire questions at him about his home life. He was a copper and acted like one all the time. Paul sat in his passenger seat with his guts turning inside out. He had a copy of *Alice in*

Wonderland with him with a hard red cover and tried to read it instead of listening to what his dad was saying. He wanted to disappear inside that book. His dad would cry all the way up and down the motorway.

He had a bedroom in both places — his mam's council house and his dad's police flat, and quite soon neither felt like his own.

He'd sit in the bath on Sunday night and his mam would fire off questions about his dad's new place, and which girlfriend he'd been seeing. On Saturday nights Paul would be at his Little Nanna's while his dad was out with a girlfriend. This was something his mam wasn't meant to know, but of course she did.

Saturday nights were festive. Granddad going out for sweets. Sausage and chips. *Doctor Who.* The late film. Very late nights. Drowsing on the settee in the smoky room.

Do all humans spend their adult years trying to re-create the happiest bits of their childhoods?

It just strikes me, because Paul spends so much of his time back inside those old *Doctor Who* episodes. He spends so much time inside all those memories.

His dad used to drop him off in Durham, halfway home on Sunday night. He remembers very foggy dark nights on Old Elvet

Bridge. Getting out of Dad's car and walking across the old stones. There was no one else about. The Cathedral looming up the hill, way above the trees. The distant sound of the green river below.

His dad would watch from his car until Mam appeared, from the other side. In her long brown coat, with her long hair combed back. Paul would meet her in the very middle of the bridge and she'd take his hand. Her new boyfriend was parked up the winding street on the other side, in the marketplace. Her new boyfriend, Brian, who was about to move in.

Mam decided it was best if Dad and Brian were kept on opposite sides of the river like this.

Brian never spoke. He glowered and muttered and radiated bad moods all the time. He never directed a single word at Paul until Paul was about thirteen. He wouldn't be in the same room as him, or sit on the same piece of furniture.

All of these things I've picked up, piece by piece, from Paul, in the time I've lived with him. He tells Jeremy bits and pieces from the same stories in the middle of the night, over meals, and when they're sitting in the car.

"Why do you keep roving over the same

old stuff?" Jeremy asks crossly. "You're obsessed with going over and over the same things."

Paul can't explain. "It's just what I do. I suppose it's because I write . . ."

"You keep dwelling on things and making yourself miserable."

Is it really about writing? Sometimes Paul wonders about that. He tells me: "Everyone in my family roves over the same old stuff. We go over the same stories. Some of them funny, some of them horrible. But it's like nothing's really happened to us until the story's been told a dozen times."

"Ungow," I say thoughtfully. And I am thinking about it, I really am. Even though it's Christmas and it's late and we're stuffed with turkey. I can't even be bothered to move, but I'm thinking about the idea of roving over old stories. Especially the ones that make you sad. Cats don't do that, you see. Cats tend to forget. We live in the moment. That's what most cats would say. I don't see it quite like that, though. Maybe I just remember more than most.

"You really listen, don't you?" Paul asks, sounding surprised. "The way you look at me! Sometimes I really think you're taking it all in!"

And, it's true, I think, that to cats, time

itself feels as if it moves quite differently. I forget where I am in time. These quiet and slow days and nights, it's easy to become unpeeled from the surface of time. It's not that time is standing still, it's more like I'm lying still on the surface of time and being in more than one place at once.

Tonight I feel like I'm in every Christmas me and the boys will ever have together. I can see them all stretched out. Seven of them. Perfect.

I suppose Paul is thinking like this because his family is about to arrive for a couple of days. Jeremy says he stresses himself out about them. Wanting them to have a nice time, and knowing that they won't. Something will go wrong. They'll sabotage it somehow. Jeremy braces himself for the inevitable. I find these visits quite tense too. They aren't really cat people. They like dogs.

ANOTHER VISIT

They're hard to please. That's what I think. I tell Paul when he's in the kitchen, "Don't fret. Don't get worked up. Just enjoy it."

The house is too cold. There's something wrong with the boiler and the radiators need bleeding or something. He thought it was warm enough for them, but his whole family is keeping their coats on as they sit in the front room. "I'm always cold," his mam says. The stepfather sits on one side, glowering, and his sister sits on the other, scowling.

The sister is in her twenties now and Paul can hardly believe it. She's so much younger than he is. He expected her to be a baby forever. The whole family did. Right now she just wants to go to Primark to buy some tops. She's not bothered about this visit. She just likes the shops in Manchester. She'll be happier if they can get downtown and get into Primark, which is a big shop with discount clothes.

I hop onto my blanket on the smaller settee and watch them.

Paul's mam had to be helped into the house. I wasn't expecting that. I'd picked up from Paul the fact that she's ill, but I wasn't prepared for how it would be. She held on to her husband's arm as they walked from their car to the house and over the tall step. Every step is a real battle for her. She is dreading needing the toilet here because there isn't one downstairs. Somehow she'll have to deal with the stairs.

They're talking about the hotel they're staying in. Paul found them somewhere not too far away. They're talking about breakfast. He's telling them to just have what they want.

"Well, I won't have anything. Just some dry toast. I don't eat much," says his mam.

"If you want a Full English, Brian, Louise, then you just tell them," says Paul. But they both look away from him. Somehow he's offended them, and he's not sure how. Possibly because he only paid in advance for Continental. But they'd rather have bacon and stuff. Well, frankly, so would I. And I can tell that the more he's going on about it, the worse he's making it.

"Louise paid for the dogs to go in the kennels for two nights," his mam points out. "The prices are shocking. I had a row on the phone with the woman. We can't afford to pay it. Luckily Louise helped us out."

"I'm sorry they can't come here," Paul says. Secretly, he's relieved. The dogs are sweet but they haven't been trained. The smaller one barks constantly and it wears the nerves down. "It's Fester's house now," he says. "He'd hate having dogs around." I feel a little swell of pride at that. Fester's house.

"When you get animals they take over your life," his mam says. "Worse than having kids." Louise tuts and his mam laughs. "Only joking! I didn't mean you, Louise.

You're my little gift from heaven."

"Huh," says Louise. Somehow even the way she's sitting seems to say she can't be bothered with being here. She glances around at all the odd and mismatched stuff in the boys' front room. The others are looking too, and muttering things to each other when Paul and Jeremy leave the room.

"You could have this house so lovely," Paul's mam tells him. "It'll be nice when it's all done up. You're so lucky."

They have dinner and it's a battle to get them to eat. "We don't really eat much," Mam says, and she means "food like this." They all pick at what he's cooked. He's steamed salmon for them and I can barely restrain myself. With the whole lot of them here there's not a spare chair for me to hop onto. I sit hopefully in the doorway, glorying in the smell of dinner.

"Your cat's a bit noisy," his mam says. "What's he called again?"

"Fester."

"Why did you call him that? And who did you say he belongs to?"

Paul laughs. "The Spanish woman up the street, but she doesn't want him anymore. He came looking for us."

"What Spanish woman?"

Paul and Jeremy tell the story again, all

192

about the woman who turned out not to be Spanish, and her runaway cat who turned out not to be a girl. No one laughs. They just look at me, frowning.

"It's a skinny little thing. It looks like a girl," says Mam.

"It's got eyeliner all round its eyes," says Louise. "And look! It's got a Hitler moustache! Hahahahaha!"

"Hurr hurr hurr," says Brian.

"It's a Kitler!" says Louise. "That's what they call cats with Hitler moustaches. There's a whole website about it. People send in pictures. Can I send one of him? Hahahaha!"

Paul frowns. "Er, no thanks."

"Louise," Mam says. "Don't be awful. What do you mean, Kitler? I don't understand what she's on about. It's a lovely cat, aren't you? The things you think up, Louise, honestly."

"Hurr, hurr, hurr." Brian laughs.

Later, they open presents in the front room. Swapping wrapped gifts and exclaiming over things. I enjoy being amongst all that for a while, messing with the crumpled paper and ribbons. It's a chance too for Paul and his mam to get nostalgic and repeat a few old stories about Christmases past. Just a few mentions here and there. Not great long storytelling sessions like Paul usually goes in for. It's more like, "Eeh, remember when?" or "When was that time when . . . ?"

There's a bag of presents gone missing. "I'm sure we had another bag of stuff. Brian? Brian? Where did that other bag go? But there *was* more . . . I'm sure of it . . ."

Paul tries to say that he doesn't mind about presents. She doesn't have to worry. All her life she's fretted about buying enough, giving enough. Not just at Christmas. Birthdays and other times. It's like his mam has spent her whole life trying to make up for something. Trying to make things better with these little toys and gifts. He tries to say that the best thing is that they are here. That they can have another Christmas night like this, together, a couple of days after Boxing Day. But it comes out wrong. Or she takes it the wrong way, and she looks like he's said he doesn't care for his gifts from her.

Out in the back garden, Brian and Jeremy are smoking in the dark. I pad out to see what's going on. They're talking out here and smoking two cigarettes each, one after another. Jeremy is making a huge effort to make Brian talk. Paul is grateful because Brian never talks to anyone. He never has. It was always a mistake to even try. But

Jeremy doesn't care about any of that. He doesn't care about anyone's past, or habits, or what might offend them. He just weighs in and starts chatting brightly. Sociably. Often about manly topics like house repairs, gardening, or cars. It's how he behaves with everyone and I can sense how pleased and relieved Paul is. It's always been like that. Jeremy can be relied upon to do this kind of thing. To make things easier.

The patio is strung with fairy lights. So are the bushes in the back garden. It's like a Christmas grotto. I head off to what the boys laughingly call Poo Corner and do a swift one and cover it up with hard earth.

The cold out here is delicious. But only because I know I don't have to stay out in it.

Host

A day later and it's the boys' Christmas party. It's only their second Christmas in this house, but it's a tradition now. They throw a modest shindig every year on the same day, just before New Year.

If you add up the seven Christmases we have together, that's a lot of guests all jostling for space in their crowded, cluttered-up house. That's a lot of old vinyl records spinning on the turntable — a lot of Abba, a lot of disco classics. It's a huge number of nibbles, brought out of the oven on baking trays — roasted pink prawns and curls of bacon and spicy sausages. A great many glasses of pink and bubbly wine.

I can see all of those nights now, one overlapping the next — and I can see myself coming down the stairs, woken up by the rising noise levels. I thread my way down the hallway and into the kitchen, weaving through their legs and shouting up at people

I recognise. The neighbours and friends recognise me and call out my name. I'm making an entrance. I'm carrying on as if the party is in my honour.

I try to pounce onto the kitchen table, but Paul's laying out salads and crisps and cheese and stuff. I guess he's not keen on having me bumming up all his buffet. I check out my feeding station and there's a decent cat buffet laid out there in different dishes.

Mackerel pâté. Now, that's what I call party food.

In the front room it's all a bit of a squash. I can see some of my favourites — Deborah and Jamie and Alicia, Caroline, Nick, Karen and Mark. And a few of my lesser favourites. Albert and Jasmine, for example. Everyone's talking at the tops of their voices because Tina Charles is singing "Dr. Love" at full blast. Someone's sitting on Fester's seat, of course, but I guess that's okay when there's a whole houseful.

Paul comes in and out with dishes and stuff, checking that everyone's having fun. Sometime after ten it all steps up a gear and all the shyness and awkwardness suddenly fades. Maybe they're all a bit tipsy suddenly, or maybe they can relax at last. This happens the same, every year. Some latecomers turn up — Wayne and Iain, and one or two more. There's a lot of laughing and singing.

I go round a few conversations and look up at who's talking. Some of them are disconcerted by how I study them. They think I'm after food or something, or a pat on the head. But I'm not, really. I'm just taking part.

"He's, er, very talkative," says one woman I don't recognise. Someone from Paul's university, maybe. She's noticed how I'm going, "Mow! Mow mow! Ungow!" when there are gaps in the conversation she's having with Jamie.

Then I go round and try out a few knees. Some folk are more welcoming and comfy than others. I visit my favourites and devote a few minutes to each in turn. I go round saying hellos in my own way. Bit of chin rubbing, a bit of nudging.

I'm a pretty good host, actually.

And when I've decided that enough's enough, I totter up the wooden hill to bed.

Best thing about being a cat at a party? Second only to the prawns?

No washing up. No tidying.

I'm first in bed and I sleep happily, ears twitching, still half listening to a houseful of disco tunes and friends.

198

BESSY MOVES IN

With the sun comes longer days, and the back door is open to the garden. And someone is stealing my food.

"My God, there's two of them!" Paul says.

Jeremy's reading the *Guardian* at the table outside. "Hmm?"

"There's another Fester, in the kitchen," Paul says. "I mean, another black-and-white cat, eating from Fester's bowl."

I'm on the patio, basking in the sun, and at the sound of my name I shake myself awake and sit upright. Another Fester? What's he on about? Already I'm annoyed.

Paul goes back into the kitchen and stands by my feeding station, staring at the rather large black-and-white cat who has put her whole face into my orange bowl. She's eating ravenously.

I proceed with caution up the steps and into my kitchen.

She turns to look at us. Her whole body is

braced, ready to flee. She gives off her usual belligerent vibes. But actually, I'm dead pleased to see her. At first, anyway. "Bessy!"

She must have snuck up the garden, across the patio, and into the house without anyone seeing. She always was a proper slyboots.

Paul is staring at her. She's got a blob of cat food on her pink nose. Now that he looks, he can see that she hardly resembles me at all. "Where did you come from?" he asks her. "Hey? When did you let yourself in?"

Bessy shoots me a glance. "What a loser. Does he talk to you like that as well? Does he treat you like you're soft?" She nibbles a bit more at the remains of my midmorning snack.

"He's all right," I tell her. "Don't you go slagging him off, lady. Paul and Jeremy have been very good to me."

"Yeah, yeah," she says, yawning suddenly, revealing that huge mouth of hers and its full, frightening array of fangs. "Wow, I'm shagged out. Where do I sleep?"

"Huh?"

"They've made you dopey and slow, Fester. All this luxury. You've gone soft in the head. I said, where do I sleep? I'd rather have my own space. I don't want to go lying anywhere you've spread all your scent about. Where's good? Upstairs? Downstairs? In my ladies' chamber?"

She turns her back on Paul and slinks into the hallway, sniffing about and looking up at the banisters.

I follow. "What are you on about, you daft old tart?"

"Isn't it obvious?" She grins. "You've got a new houseguest. Probably for quite a while. Your old aunty Bessy has come to stay! I'm moving in, Fester Cat!"

My heart plummets into the soles of my feet. "What?! But . . . you can't! You can't just move in. They'll never let you."

She shrugs those big shoulders of hers and puffs out her buxom white chest. "I think you'll find they already have. I'm hard to get out, once I'm over the threshold."

Now she's trotting to the bottom of the staircase and peering up. "Huh. These stairs could do with a good hoover. Are they not very house proud, these two?"

"Bessy . . . !"

I chase after her, but she's dashing up the stairs, two at a time.

Downstairs Paul's been distracted by something. He's messing on with the oven. He's doing something for lunch. He turns the radio up. It's almost the Disco Lunch

201

Hour. I can hear the pounding beat coming up through the floorboards. He thinks it's just the same as any other day. But it isn't. We've got an interloper.

ROUGH

Bessy smells a bit widdly and fusty, like she's been living somewhere not very nice lately.

"It's been a long, hard winter," she tells me. "Fierce. Some of them guys out there, they'd rip your head off just to get your dinner off you. I've never known it so cutthroat round there."

She's lolling on the leopard-skin cushions on top of the blanket box. This is right in front of the window in the boys' bedroom, and the midday sun comes gently through the net curtains. She stretches out, looking all elegant and poised. She sighs deeply.

I'm sitting on the boys' rumpled bed, watching her, still half dumb with shock at her sudden appearance. Her acrid scent fills the room.

"You've landed on your feet here, Fester." She snickers. "I always knew you would. You and that daft Korky. I always knew you were pampered house cats, really. I knew you were a pair of softies. Well, you chose right this winter, Fester. I feel half dead with scratting a living. So that's why I'm setting my foolish pride aside for once, and I'm coming to stay with you."

"But . . . !" I gasp. I always feel young and stupid when I'm talking to Bessy. She makes me feel so unsettled and unsure. "But the fellas don't want another cat, I'm sure of it. I mean, they weren't really looking for a cat at all. I just sort of happened into their lives."

Bessy nods, her pale green eyes look calculating, just as I remember. "You did a good job, I reckon. Getting them to take you in. A raggy old thing like you. Proper state, you were in. You'd never have hacked it on the streets without them. And look at you now. You're looking pretty good, Fester. Not to puff you up too much, but you're in pretty fine shape."

I look down, determined not to be flattered by her. Bessy has a way of wrapping you round her claws and getting just what she wants from you.

I really thought I'd seen the last of her.

She doesn't even ask about Korky, or any of the others. I guess she's been keeping tabs on us all and already knows all the news.

"H-how long will you stay?"

"Spring, perhaps?" she muses. "Maybe longer? We'll see. You'll share your space and food and things with old Aunty Bessy, won't you?" She grins at me, spreading herself out on the blanket box. "I mean, you're not going to go all territorial on me, are you, daft lad? Let's face it. We're both strays, really, aren't we? You just got yourself this cushy number first."

I can see that she's got herself pretty determined about staying here. I turn — feeling pretty miserable — and hurry back downstairs.

"Paaaauuu-aaarrrruuaaallll?" I call, and he's putting out their food. Beans on toast. Pretty boring.

"Fester," he says as Jeremy comes in to be fed. "Where did that other cat go? Did you chase it out?"

I pad heavily over to my feeding station. My dish is almost empty and it reeks of her. I sigh. "She says she's stopping," I tell the boys.

But they don't realise yet what she's like. They don't know what has got into their house.

GUMS

I don't know why they're being so soft on her.

There's been no discussion, no big decision. I don't think she's actually, officially moved in, but neither have they booted her out, either.

The boys haven't actually adopted Bessy in the way they did me. I mean, why would they? She's not lovable. She's not even very nice. She's not entertaining and she makes absolutely zero effort at getting along with people. She just sits around the place with her chest puffed out and her green eyes blazing at anyone who comes near. She eats half the cat food and has let it be known that, really, being bigger than me, she should have more than I get.

I'm not best pleased, let's put it that way.

At least she's not sleeping over. That's one thing. Last thing each night, when he goes round locking up and switching off all the lamps, Paul hoists her up in one hand and takes her to the front door. "Come on, Bessy. Time to go a-hunting."

Each time I breathe a long sigh of relief.

Funny how, when one of the humans picks her up, she goes all limp and weightless. She looks like a fur stole or something, hanging from his hand. Strange, when you know how much fierce and independent spirit is bound up in that slinky cat body. But, as I say, she's sly. When she's with the boys she's like, "Oh, I'm just a poor starving alley cat who's fallen on hard times. You guys need to feed me up and give me a home and stuff."

When we're alone Bessy laughs at them behind their backs. "They're such a pushover. You've got them well trained, Fester. They're real softies. I wonder if it's because they're gay men?" she muses. "Maybe they're starved of familial affection because of their decadent lifestyle? What do you think? Maybe they're just needy?"

I think about that Albert and his "unmet needs." I hate the snarling cynicism in Bessy's voice. It isn't like that round here at all. Bessy will see, I think. If she hangs around she will see the truth about them.

But really, she's just a bit of a user.

They buy special biscuits for her to crunch

on with all her long, white teeth. She sits in the kitchen, doing this with relish and making wisecracks about my own dental situation.

"How did you smash all your teeth out, Fester?" She snickers. "I think I might have known at one point. Didn't you tell me?"

"I can't remember," I say, keeping my mouth tight shut. When I do that it forms a wonky straight line and I know it betrays how peevish I'm feeling.

"Didn't you lose them in a cat-flap incident? Or was it because you were chasing after cars in the street?" She shrugs. "No matter. But you do look funny with your single fang."

I've got more than one fang. She hasn't even looked at me properly, the dozy mare.

My gums hurt and they feel swollen all the time. Sometimes I draw the boys' attention with the noises I make when I'm eating. They can tell my damaged mouth causes me pain.

They talk with Mr. Joe the hairdresser about the possibilities and he decides yes, in the months I've been living here, I've built up my strength and my resilience. I've been on a good diet and I'm no longer the wretched creature I was. If we want to think about surgery on my gums now, then we should go ahead.

I don't hear all the grisly details. But it's a big, proper operation, for which I'll have to have a general anaesthetic. The worry before was that I might never wake up from such a heavy dose. I might sink so deeply into sleep I could never get back out again. But we all trust Mr. Joe when he says that I should be all right now. Though it's always a risk with surgery like this, the operation if successful would make a big difference to me and my comfort.

The details are awful. He will cut open all my gums and get out all the tender, rotting stumps of tooth that are still there and caus-ing me pain. Then I will be stitched up again. It'll take a lot of time and I will have to stay away from home overnight in a cage at the hairdresser's.

I'm so dazed by all the details that I don't think I take them in at all.

Bessy waves me off on Monday morning from the front doorstep.

"See yer, Fester. Wouldn't want to be yer."

Paul waves Jeremy off as he manhandles my carrying case into the Škoda. I've got a new, very trendy case Jeremy bought in the Selfridges sale. It's dove grey with a powder-blue base. It's very swanky.

I'm sitting inside on a small blue blanky,

with one or two mouse-shaped toys for comfort. I've never really seen much point in toys and usually refuse to play with them, or even acknowledge them.

But sitting in my carry case in the passenger seat as the car veers down backstreets to the Stockport Road, I do find these little fellas a comfort. I hold the pink glittery one under my left paw and squeeze my claws around him, very gently.

OVERNIGHT

I'm lucky because I'm not aware of much that goes on while I'm at the hairdresser's. It's Mr. Joe who has all the hard work to do. And it's the boys who stay awake worrying about me for much of that night.

They think about me being completely zonked and under bright lights on the operating table. They think about the dangers that Mr. Joe outlined.

All I really know about it is sitting on the hairdresser's table when we first arrive and saying hello to Mr. Joe. He always seems surprised when I'm as cheery as I am. I even say "Ungow" to him.

And, later, I seem to be aware of being put into one of their cages. But they're quite roomy. It smells peculiar. Other cats and medicine and stuff. Clean, though. Too clean, if anything. But I've got my blanky and my glittering mouse, and really, I'm too tired to think about anything else.

At home they put out Bessy for the night. Apparently she has sat there glaring at the two of them all evening while they fretted about me. I can just imagine it.

"Hey, if he karks it — you've still got me. I'm better than him. I've got perfect teeth."

I bet she was slinking around that front room while I was gone. I bet she was rolling around on her back, puffing out her chest and shouting for a tummy tickle. I hope they didn't bother. I hope they noticed her great big bollocks and realised she isn't actually the lady she pretends to be.

I bet she even tried to sit in my spot in front of the fire. Or on the two-seater settee or in my basket. I bet she was trying to muscle in on all my favourite places.

Anyhow, forget Bessy.

I've enough of my own stuff to think about.

For the next morning I wake up muzzily in a place I don't recognise. I can hear the breathing and mewling of other animals. I shrink back into my cage and my mouth feels odd. I'm not sure if I hurt or not. I just feel very weird. There's like a vast white cloud inside my head, squashing all my thoughts down, muffling everything I can feel.

The nice nurse comes in and brings food

and stuff. They come and have a look at me. Time passes. And more time passes. I sleep for a bit, even though it's quite bright in here and my mouth doesn't feel quite normal.

And then they come to carry me out and I'm in Mr. Joe's room again. He's there and it's first thing in the morning. The start of a new day and Mr. Joe smiles like he's incredibly pleased with me.

And then . . . oh, and then . . . Jeremy's there!

He's walking in, swinging my Selfridges carry case. He's grinning and standing over me and pushing his huge face right up to mine. I'm still feeling a bit weak and woozy. I strain with every bit of strength to push myself forward to nudge my face against his. *Boop! Boop!* But I can't. Mr. Joe says I'm exhausted and sore. I need to recover. I've been through quite a lot for one little cat.

I've had surgery!

They bundle me gently into the carry case and there's lots of chat going over my head. It takes some time and then, eventually, we're out of the hairdresser's. I call out "Ungow" to Mr. Joe and the nice ladies, but I'm not sure they hear me. The cold of the street outside hits me and feels a bit sore on my mouth.

But then we're in the car. We're going home.

Fester Cat is coming home in triumph!

We made it! I made it!

I'm coming home again!

CRUNCH

There's a lot of chewing goes on after this.

All of a sudden there's no pain when I eat. I'd become so used to it. I thought it was just part of life now. I'd have to eat very slowly and carefully, bolting my food and trying not to chew. But Mr. Joe took all of that nasty stuff out of my gums. All the dead stumps of teeth and the built-up plaque. Stuff I'd rather not think about.

And I can chew what I want.

I've still only got one and a half teeth, but I can chomp and mash them down on slightly tougher cat food than before. And, best of all, I can crunch biscuits. Paul and Jeremy try me out on special biscuits for cats. Tiny, savoury things, some of them with creamy fish or meat inside the brittle shells. I get them in exactly the right part of my mouth, between my bits of teeth, and crunch them like mad.

It's all very satisfying.

Bessy sits there, looking impressed despite herself. "Well, I must admit, they've done you a good turn there, Fester. They must think something of you after all."

I just smile at her. My lip still catches on my tooth and so my grin's still lopsided. But I couldn't imagine that being any different now. It's just part of my whole look.

A whole, wonderful world of chewing has opened up.

I used to have to swallow things whole. Those bits of bacon and ham and whatnot. Now I mash them into nothing and everything tastes even more wonderful. Already I'm wondering about hunting. What about mice and birds and all that stuff? Flying and

216

creeping takeaways, as Bessy calls them. I wonder if I'll have a go at trapping and chomping and crunching up some small, wild creatures? Maybe now that the weather's improved I could slip out for a few nights and try my luck by the railway tracks?

Bessy and I venture out and we lurk in smelly undergrowth and pad about in the dripping recesses beneath the railway lines.

After my months of comfort these places seem very strange and dangerous to me. I'm not even that far from home. We're just in the grassy embankment at the end of Chestnut Avenue, but my heart is pounding. I can smell foxes. I can hear them. That desolate yelping as the hunting hours begin. The church clock strikes midnight on the Stockport Road. I can hear the endless shushing of traffic going into town and out again. The vast rushing roar of the trains above our heads. It's exhilarating, but maybe it's too much for me.

Usually, by this time of night, I'm on my blanky, in my basket, curled up, half aware of TV, and dozing with the boys.

Bessy snickers and points out a chattering cloud of tiny bats circling the last house on the terrace. "Oh, imagine grabbing one of those little monsters." She sighs. "Have you ever had a bat, Fester? Very hard to catch,

217

but worth it. Tastes a lot like vole."

Everything in the darkness seems alive. The wet grass is shriekingly alive as we pass through its tangles. The branches and all their new buds are singing with colour I can still see in the dark. The mulchy ground seethes with insects and worms and the grubbing activities of the underground mice and moles. Bessy is way ahead of me, I'm even losing her scent. She's laughing like the spring night is making her a bit unhinged.

This brings back those months and years I spent living out here, and worse places. All of that had started to slip from my memory. Already my fur starts to itch at the memory of the sores and scabs I always wore. My new, painless gums start to throb with remembered ache.

I want to go home.

This isn't for me anymore.

The fox yowls again. It can smell us, maybe. We used to play such games baiting him and his wife. I can't remember now what we were doing it for. Just passing the time, I guess. We were pretty wild in those days, running up and down the embankment.

Bessy's leading the way up top. I remember how she used to love to run across the railway tracks.

"It's the thrill of it, yeah. But it's also the wonderful smells you encounter. It's like the way underneath a car smells. All that oily tang and exhaust fumes and stuff. And the scents of faraway places bound up in that burned rubber and hot, smouldered metal. The railway tracks and the stones up there smell the same but a hundred times more strong. And there's dead birds and all sorts. You should come, Fester! Come up top!"

Once or twice in the old days I crossed the railway tracks at Levenshulme station with her. I was foolish for doing that. It was stupidly dangerous. She used to play daredevil with the trains rushing out to Heaton Chapel, Stockport, Alderley Edge. Her game was to stand in the middle of the tracks while the automated lady read out lists of towns through the tall speakers. We knew the trains were coming then. She'd stand there, sniffing up the tracks, putting the pink pads of her paws on the vibrating metal. She would wait until the last few moments and then dive into the siding.

I did it only a couple of times over those years. I didn't like it very much.

Most of my time was spent in the deep undergrowth, sniffing at the rubbish and the dead stuff and the old food chucked where no one could find it.

My life was nowhere near as good back then. Bessy can romanticize all she wants.

She calls me again, and I can tell that she's up on the tracks. I'm not going there tonight.

I turn and leave her to it.

I make my own way back through the matted jungle to the terrace. It's after midnight. I'm hoping the boys haven't locked up already.

But when I get to the street I can hear a familiar jingle-jangle. Even before I get close enough to see the house, I know what's happening. I know that the jangling is Paul shaking his bundle of house keys in his hand.

There he is. The front door's open. The hall light spills out on the gravel. He's in his cardy and striped pyjamas, looking tired. He looks like he needs a little cat to lie on his duvet while he reads. *Jingle-jangle.* "Fester ca-aa-aat?"

I wonder if he's been calling for long? But I've heard him now.

I go running to him.

He catches sight of me just as I'm bounding down the middle of the road, my mouth set in a wonky, determined line.

HEY, MANHATTAN

They aren't always at home. Sometimes they go away.

They go away and they leave out plenty of food for me. They draw all the curtains so the house is dusky all day long. Neighbours come by to top up my dishes and sometimes they spend a little time with me. Karen visits and I sit with her for a while, just when I'm feeling the need for company. Mostly when they're away I doze. I make the most of the peace.

Nick from down the street comes round and he tunes the radio for me. He says I like variety. I like voices talking in the morning on Radio 4. Then he switches it to Radio 3 in the afternoon, because he says I like some calming music then. He's pretty accurate with that, actually. I enjoy the way these neighbours take turns, coming by to open a food pouch or to fill my water glass. I greet them with a cheery "Ungow."

Where is my family when all of this is going on? Paul and Jeremy have tried to explain to me the kinds of places they go to.

They catch taxis early in the mornings on the days they set off. They load up these cars with their heavy bags and I sit on Paul's desk, staring out of his study window, watching it all going on. I can sense when the departure days are coming and I know I'll have a few days on my own. When they're packing their cases on the bed I've jumped in once or twice, as if they'll zip me up and take me with them. When they go off without me I can't help feeling just a little sulky.

The airport is only a few miles away. The planes often come over our street quite low as they skim under the clouds, streaking over Levenshulme, Stockport, Cheadle, and towards Manchester Airport. From up there you can even see the Stockport Road, Paul says. "When we're taking off or coming in to land, we'll see the house, Fester. We'll see our roof and we'll know you're waiting for us down there."

I'm not sure I believe in the whole business of flying. I can understand it intellectually and I know it must happen. And, of course, I've paid close attention to a great many birds. I've watched magpies and thrushes, pigeons and geese flapping over our garden. Once a year there's a heron who pauses for breath on next door's roof. A heron is a startling sight for a cat. Like an elegant turkey on stilts.

I can't imagine what it must be like, flying.

Similarly, I feel like the places they talk about going to — they're all made up as well. They bring back souvenirs, presents, photos of themselves that they frame and put on our walls or in books or on Facebook. But it might as well all be stories, as far as I'm concerned. Nevertheless, I love hearing them.

The longest trip they made, leaving me here at home, was when they went to New York — and it was more than two weeks. This was for Jeremy's new job, when he was involved in a huge conference to do with education. He said it was thousands of people, all staying in hotels in the middle of the city that never sleeps.

Before they went we watched films so they and I could see where they were going — *Annie Hall, Spider-Man, Valley of the Dolls*. I couldn't take in how huge it was, of course. The city was shining glass and brown stone and vast green gardens.

Paul wandered up and down the endless

city streets while Jeremy worked at his conference. Paul went to see huge splashy paintings, dinosaur skeletons, and snow monkeys. He went to Greenwich Village for coffee and wrote in his notebook. He found bookshops specializing in murder mysteries and gay stuff, and a pet shop with a window full of excited puppies. He had a reunion — after eighteen years — with his first-ever boyfriend. They went for a walk around Central Park, wandering through the zoo and talking about 1990, when they were both twenty. They shared the same birthday, the same love of writing, and of cats. They shared book chat and cat gossip.

Later, Paul told me all of this and none of it surprised me. Cats always expect synchronicity and coincidence. I've said it before. Cats expect the world to rhyme.

The boys told me about going to see a show on Forty-second Street, sitting high in the gods for a revival of Paul's favourite musical, *Gypsy*. They talked about being at MoMA and looking at Matisse while Jeremy phoned for news of me and heard from Nick about my radio-listening preferences.

They talked about picking up soup and crackers, sandwiches and coffee and sitting by the duck pond together. And eavesdropping quietly on all the drama going on around them.

Seems to me sometimes that when they go away they do such ordinary things. It's the same as all the stuff they do at home.

Then they both came down with a horrible flu bug. It being an international conference, there was a lot of world-class germs about. Their last few, free days in the city they were deliriously sick, lying about in their suite at the top of an overheated hotel on Seventh Avenue. Hardly able to move. They went out eventually to the Carnegie Deli to pick up burgers and cheesecake and could hardly manage a bite.

They were glad to set off for home. The journey was so arduous it felt like they crawled all the way back.

I was there when the car pulled up outside our house at six in the morning. I was already awake, knowing something different was going to happen that day. I shoved my head between the curtains and saw them staggering out of their taxi in the first light.

They just about fell indoors.

I watched them — cautious, incredulous. They were back! And what a state the pair of them were in. What had they done to themselves? At first I was worried.

Then I decided I was in a huff with them. Both of them. They'd abandoned me.

They'd been gallivanting about in New York. Served them right if they came back feeling rotten.

I stayed in a huff for about a day. They were so busy being ill they hardly noticed. They fed me and cleaned up the litter trays. They opened all the windows and the back door and let Bessy out. She vanished gladly into the wilderness for a few days. During their trip she had been out and about when neighbours called. She had been no bother to me. I'd been a bit worried about being stuck with her, but Bessy had retreated into herself. Nowadays she had her own places and perches about the house and they were quite different from mine. Our paths really only crossed at mealtimes.

I luxuriated in being outside again. The air was soft and cool. I had a scamper round all the corners of our garden and watched the trains go by, and the planes. It was after Easter and spring was everywhere. New and interesting stuff was poking out of the ground and bushes. The pale pink buds of the magnolia were poised to open. The young squirrels were brazen. They shinned down from their dreys high atop the beech tree and chased each other along the fences for the sheer hell of it.

I was glad the boys were back. I couldn't

stay mad at them for long.

I announced the end of my sulk the following day, when they were rested. They were both woozily back on their feet. Jeremy had lost most of his voice.

"Ungow," I told them. It was my way of saying — "Okay, forgiven and everything. Just don't stay away as long as that again. Never again. Don't start me off worrying about the pair of you. Now, come on. Come and sit outside in the sun with Fester Cat. Tell me all about your New York adventures."

I went to the warm patio and flomped on my back, letting them take turns to tickle me daft.

PANDA

There's one other person in our house that I haven't talked about. That's because I'm not even sure he's a person. The way Jeremy and Paul talk about him it's as if he's a person. But he's not. Not really. At least, not in the normal way.

Some people can't deal at all with Panda.

That Albert, for one, looks dismayed whenever Panda comes into the room and starts talking to him. He once turned to Paul — when they were all out for dinner in town — and said, "I don't have time for this." He meant that Panda was insisting on carrying on a conversation with him and he was embarrassed. Life was too short to be seen talking with a stuffed toy in public.

That's what Panda is. A ten-inch-tall stuffed toy. Except both he and Jeremy would be scandalized to hear you say it. He's as much a part of the household as the rest of us, and has been for quite some time.

Most people simply accept him. Most people engage him in chitchat. The first time I was aware of it, I was flabbergasted. Why are they talking to a toy bear?

"Bear . . . ?!"

Then I was made aware that pandas are not actually bears. At least, according to Panda.

"Bears are nasty, stinky, rather wild things, Fester," Panda told me. "And as I hope you can tell, I am nothing of the sort. I'm a highly respectable Panda and an Art Critic at that. I review ballet and opera for the more serious-minded broadsheets . . ."

And so he goes on. Holding forth. Pontificating. Airing his opinions to all and sundry. Paul and Jeremy never seem to go anywhere without him. He commutes everywhere in Jeremy's shoulder bag and has his own seat in the back of their car.

"What?" Bessy said, shocked, when she first moved in. "What is this? What are they up to?"

Panda gave her quite a hard look. He boggled at her. Which meant he shook his head at her quite severely.

"He's their friend," I told Bessy.

She didn't look very impressed. "Freaks."

Panda's been everywhere with them. He was with them when they went to New York. He's been to Paris with them several times. "Ah, la Paree," he exclaims. "Yes, I know it very well, of course. It's the only place that those two will ever go on holiday. But, of course, I knew it in the old days, hanging around the cafés with the old Existentialist fellows . . ."

I'd say that Panda lives in a complete fantasy world. He burbles on like this for hours.

He claims to have lived with them since the millennium. He "moved in with them" in Christmas 1999. Though I gather Paul bought him from a shop somewhere in Norfolk. He was a present for Jeremy, who had had a panda ever since he was extremely small. That old panda was worn away to almost nothing. But when the current fin-de-siècle panda came home with them, they got more than they bargained for. He started to speak. To have loud and complicated opinions.

Of course, I know it's one of the boys doing his voice, whenever he does actually speak. That hectoring, fruity voice isn't actually coming from Panda himself. I know they're just playing a game.

"Isn't this marvellous, Fester?" he bellow

at me from his deck chair in the overgrown grass. "This whole garden to ourselves! And all this sun! I can tell it's going to be a wonderful summer, this year."

I'm slinking about in the grass, sniffing here and there. I wish Panda would shut up and just go back to reading his book.

"In the last place they lived they never had a garden, of course," says Panda. "When they lived in that little flat in town. There was no garden space at all. Just concrete and a car park. If they wanted to get the sun and air they'd have to get right out and walk about Castlefield or go into town, or get into the car and drive to the countryside. But this is fantastic, isn't it? We've got this whole garden like a wilderness. We could stay here all summer and never get bored . . ."

I listen when Panda tells me bits about their lives previous to moving to our street. I can't help but be fascinated by these tales. I find it hard to imagine them in other places and being there without me.

Panda even talks about when they lived in their house in Norwich, when Paul was working at the university. Panda expands on some of the characters that he met there, and the people he got to know.

"Of course, that all seems like a different

life now. A change of location can change everything. This is a much more quiet life. Paul was out all the time then, working and dashing about. Now he's only half time, teaching and things. That's why he's at home so much."

And I'm glad he is. I like sitting with him at his desk while he works.

He comes home exhausted from teaching.

Whatever this teaching business is, it seems to leave him completely drained. He's excited and disappointed at the very same time, after every session. He's out all day and evening on his teaching days. Jeremy goes to pick him up, late at night, from this place called MMU in the middle of town. Panda goes with him and they return with Paul, who looks shattered.

"Oh yes," Panda says. "He takes it all very seriously. He really wants them to learn something. But he teaches such a very funny subject, you see. It's quite difficult. He teaches them to write their stories and novels and some would say that it isn't something you can teach."

"Ungow?"

"Exactly, Fester. Some would say that you've either got that talent or you haven't. But Paul seems to hold to his belief that there's all sorts of things you can impart to these people. Technique and so on. Or maybe just giving them space and time to develop. And being their reader and editor and so on. Oh yes, he tells me all about it, me being an Art Critic. And sometimes it's quite interesting, though he does tend to waffle on about teaching quite a lot."

He's out today. He wrote all morning at his desk and then, at the very last moment, ran out for the train at Levenshulme at lunchtime. He'll be back about ten tonight. Panda and I are sitting in the sunny garden and it's Paul that's missing.

"I think he loves teaching," Panda muses. "But there's a lot of other stuff he has to do in his job that makes it difficult. Also, it's sort of a subject that some of the people in the university don't really respect or think is useful or properly academic. Novel writing is a subject that some people don't really believe in. And, you know, it takes a lot of effort to keep doing your best — all the time, every time — when people don't quite believe in you."

Then Panda turns round in the deck chair and gives me a very beady look. "Do you know what I mean?" he says pointedly.

Sometimes he really labours his point.

I dive off into the longer grass and leave him to his book. It's a Bloomsbury biography and he's hoping, he says, for some saucy bits.

ANARCHIST

The days become wonderfully long. When he's home Paul sits outside with heaps of these papery things called dissertations and essays. He's doing something called marking, but it's quite different from what I think of as marking.

He's been at the university, proctoring an exam.

"Five hundred people, twelve different exam subjects and ten proctors, and I was the chief." He shakes his head at Jeremy. "Who's the best person to call to be in charge? A novelist." He laughs. "All that pacing up and down. And all that rigmarole. It's the opposite of everything I believe in. Right in the middle of it I wanted to shout, 'Throw all your papers in the air! Make loads of noise! Write poems! Run around!' "

"You're an anarchist," Jeremy observes.

"Not really. But I hate all of that pretend hool stuff. That's where universities are

235

going. It's all turning into the worst, un-imaginative, fascistic crap . . ."

He sighs and I jump up on the patio table to cheer him up.

We have our tea outside, it's so bright and sunny. The boys have some kind of chicken and pasta thing. The chicken is covered in pesto, but I can still manage to eat the bits I'm offered.

Panda offers to help Paul with his essay marking.

Later in the evening, as the shadows start moving in from the corners of the garden, I notice that Bessy's keeping her distance. She's at the end of the garden and looking quite mardy. I head down that way to see what's up. Doesn't she feel very well?

"This isn't my scene, Fester Cat." She scowls.

"What isn't?"

"All this suburban crap. Them with their barbecues and their pink fizzy wine and their friends. And him with his university essays and their talking bloody panda. And their arthouse movies and Radio 4. It's just not me, Fester old chum."

"But . . . but . . ." I say. I can't imagine anywhere else I'd rather be. Absolutely nowhere on earth. And here we are on perfect summer evening and it's peacefi

even if Paul is ploughing through those essays and stuff. This is perfect.

"It isn't for me," Bessy says. "And really,
those two soft lads don't really want me
around, either."

"But they've made you welcome. They've
fed you and looked after you, same as me."

"Nah," she says. "Not the same. They love
you, Fester. I never gave them any choice. I
just muscled my way in. It wasn't like the
way you moved in at all. They fell in love
with you."

"Don't be soft," I tell her, squirming,
though I know she's right. And, despite
what I'm saying, I'm starting to think that
maybe it's for the best. "Where will you go?"

"Where did I ever go? Somewhere wild.
Somewhere a bit rough. Somewhere I'll
have to scrap a bit and fight my corner. You
know that's what I'm like, Fester. It's not
really my nature to lie about in luxury all
day, talking to humans and stuffed toys and
eating out of a dish."

Yes, I think. She's right.

"Okay, then." She pauses.

I sit still, watching her.

"Okay, loser. I'm off, then."

And Bessy slinks off into the bushes.
There's the heavy noise of her scaling the
ooden fence (she's put on weight since

moving in) and then she's gone. Into the wilderness of the railway embankment.

It's only much later that night that the boys realise she's sloped off somewhere. Darkness fell ages ago and they've got fairy lights and candles in the garden. We've sat outside till midnight.

Paul scouts round one last time. "Maybe Bessy wants to stay out tonight? Perhaps she's out hunting?"

Panda pulls a face. "I dread to think what she's up to. By the way, did you ever notice that she's got a huge pair of testicles hanging down?"

Jeremy's in the kitchen, putting the kettle on.

I don't tell them yet that I think Bessy has left us for good. As Paul blows out lamps and candles and locks the back door, I'm feeling relieved. I never really wanted to be in a house with two cats. And really I knew that Bessy was just sheltering here for a while.

Over the next few nights and days it becomes apparent to everyone that Bessy isn't coming back.

The boys seem a bit glum at first. Then they realise that she was always a wilder card than me. She often went off for a day or two. And she was never, ever, really their

In the evenings we sit on the patio and the boys read and sit there happily, watching their growing garden. And I keep tabs on the nighttime passeggiata. All the cats come traipsing by, one at a time or in twos. Whisper hops over the crumbling wall and hisses some terrible things as she goes by. Three-Legged Freddie squashes himself under the blue gate and rambles around in circles, spraying widdle as he goes. Then there are others. Rowan, Scoobie, and Momo. Then less familiar ones. They all pass by and call out greetings or insults or turn their snooty noses to the heavens as they trot across our rampant lawn.

And not a night goes by when I'm not looking out for Bessy. But I think she's travelled farther down the railway tracks, to the rougher part of Levenshulme. She's probably forgetting us already. She's just that kind of cat.

BAD VIBES

The boys are having a tough time of it lately. I don't know what it is. Maybe this is a funny year or the stars are in the wrong alignment. I've been keeping my eye on the moon. Maybe some years are just like that?

Jeremy's in his study, having endless phone calls. He's got a new boss, is what I've managed to pick up. And it seems that he and the boss don't get on. Work gets sent back and he has to do it again. This boss rings up at very strange hours and sends long, peculiar messages. Jeremy is starting to get annoyed and shaken up by constant criticism.

It means we don't see him much. When Jeremy gets stressed he goes into hiding. It's a bit like cats when we're ill. We find a distant corner somewhere and push our faces into the wall. We don't want bothering. Jeremy shuts himself into his study with the door closed, smoking like a fiend. H misses his meals, he stays there all evening, he works late into the night.

It's like he's running after something that he'll never catch.

There come bangs and crashes from that room. I flinch as I run across the landing. I hurry to sit with Paul at his desk and we look at each other. "This isn't good, is it?" Paul asks. We both hate seeing Jeremy stressed.

Paul tries to drag Jeremy away from his work. Let's sit in the garden. Come on downstairs. Watch this film with us. Let's go out for dinner. We could go away for the weekend?

But all Jeremy can see is the work piling up. Every step forward is three steps back. Everything he does is returned to him with all kinds of nitpicky notes attached. "Am I going mad or is what he's saying irrelevant?" he asks Paul. "And a bit bizarre and aggressive?"

Paul can't understand what's happening, really. To him it looks as if this new bloke is just trying to undermine Jeremy. It all looks like resentment to him. It feels personal.

Paul goes away for a week at this point. He's off during a break in the university erm to teach a writing course abroad. omewhere sunny and lovely. A friend of his has organised it. He gets there okay and starts teaching and then learns that the friend seems to believe he's doing it all for free, as a favour. Paul teaches the rest of the week and comes home — furious at himself, and at everyone.

The two boys sit in the garden, being cross. I try to cheer them up.

"We must both have 'mug' tattooed on our foreheads," Jeremy says.

Albert comes round and he doesn't succeed in cheering them much. He's moved onto another new job, amazingly well paid, he says, and he's gone from something he calls the public to the private sector.

"I tell you, the whole thing's going to collapse. It's untenable. The whole world economy is about to tank."

They're all eating dinner in front of the telly. Risotto with wonderful chunks of sausage.

"And the UK is in a really dreadful state. No one really sees how bad it's going to get. This business with the banks in America. It'll have huge repercussions over here. You'll see. It'll hit us and it'll end up like the Depression. I can see just how bad it's going to be. It'll be like the dark ages. Just wait."

I'm watching him and he seems almo

gleeful about the stuff he's saying. Paul tries to listen, feeling more and more depressed.

Because Jeremy's staying at his desk so long, Paul ends up doing the same, in his own room. He's working on this year's novel and he's fretting about it. "They're going to dump me, Fester," he tells me. "My publisher, I mean. I can feel it coming. This will be the last one of mine they'll do. I'm not a bestseller. I'm not doing well enough for them."

I've never known him so worried. Usually he sits there completely happily, working away and laughing out loud at some of the things he makes up. Nothing can faze him. He handles all the complicated stuff and the bad news that occasionally comes his way — and he deals with it all quite cheerily. But now there's an anxiety there. I can sense it.

So I do my best to be supportive. I hop up on his desk and come and sit by him for photos. I make him post them on Facebook. Now everyone out there can see he's got the support of Fester Cat. I nudge him when he's working too hard. Take a break. Come and play. I sit there frowning with concentration, focusing my thoughts into his when it's time to work.

"So what are these books of yours about?"

I ask him one day. "And why are they so hard to sell?"

"Well . . ." he starts. "They're mystery books. They're about the Bride of Frankenstein setting up a B-and-B in Whitby and solving supernatural mysteries with her best friend, Effie, who lives next door."

Seems perfectly straightforward to me.

But Paul fears that he's too quirky for most people. He hates that word. "Quirky." No, he loves it really. He just dislikes the fact that people use it disparagingly. His colleagues at the university have been a bit sniffy lately about his "quirky" novels. They want to know when he'll return to writing "serious" and "meaningful" books.

At a recent university cocktail party a drunk poet asked him, "It's popular novels you write, isn't it?"

He said, "Well, yes, some people seem to like them . . ." Before realizing she actually meant "populist," meaning trashy.

Ah, there's nothing wrong with trashy, I tell him. Remember? We love trashy. Trashy is where it's at.

One of the highlights of the year, these past few years, has been when the boys make a trip to Whitby itself. They go for the Halloween weekend, when the townsfolk and visitors all dress up in Gothic mode.

and have a big party. The local bookshop puts on an event for Paul and he gives a reading to an audience of Brenda and Effie fans. Many are dressed up. They come back each year to get the next book in the series signed by him. All of them are very nice to him, and Jeremy — and Panda.

I wish I could go to these things. But it seems a bit far to go in the Škoda.

I just have to imagine what such trips are like.

Though Facebook is good. And I've got my own page.

Now I can see what these people are like, in the wider world. I can see what they're up to and pictures of their adventures. It's all very interesting. Paul and Jeremy help me post updates about what I'm up to as well.

As it turns out, as time goes by, I've got my own fans on there too. I've got friends out there in the world beyond our house, our street. I've got friends beyond Manchester, in places I can't even imagine.

THE BEACH HOUSE

One of the best things that happens is the arrival of the Beach House. Or, as it soon becomes known, Fester's House.

Everyone knows that I love a sunny day. I lie on my front, white side up, and then on my back, with my black fur absorbing all the heat and light I can get. I even get a tan! Did you know black-and-white cats can tan? Patches of my fur burn to a blazing red, just at the tips. I look like I've faded from being left out in the sun.

But sometimes I get too parched and hot and need somewhere to shelter. Imagine my delight when the Beach House arrives.

I know the boys have been up to something, because they look like they're waiting for a special delivery. There is a patch been cleared in the garden. A large area of concrete at the very bottom of the garden that was once a carport. Jeremy has planted new trees and bushes, giving our garden more privacy.

Then a lorry appears one day, with the name of a garden centre near Macclesfield down one side. It pulls up at the front of the house and men go back and forth, carrying large wooden walls and planks and other bits up and down the side alley. They work hard all morning and I sit on the brick wall and watch them at it.

Whisper from next door slinks by, raising her eyebrows. "What are you lot getting, then?" she asks. Her owners are in the alley, messing with their motorbikes. Their Alsatian, Ziggy, barks madly behind their fence, desperate to see. And Three-Legged Freddie oes round in circles, he's so excited, though he's not sure why.

The men are building a house. After a while it's pretty plain to see.

It comes in fifteen parts and they assemble it quite rapidly. No nonsense. I go to sit with Paul on the backdoor steps as he has his coffee and watches progress. "Just wait and see, Fester." He grins at me.

Jeremy's taking mugs of tea out to the men and they pause.

The Beach House is wide, with four long windows, two doors, and a veranda. It's a huge thing. Big enough for several humans to live in, probably. It faces the magnolia tree and the railway lines, and lies under the shadows of the tall trees at the very bottom of the garden.

As soon as I see it, I'm in love with it.

By teatime the men are finished and the lorry has gone. The Beach House is standing there, with its doors open, ready for us to examine it.

"Ungow . . . !"

I'm laying claim to it straightaway.

Inside it smells wonderfully of new wood and sap and all sorts of interesting, faraway scents.

The two boys spend some time dragging out bits of old furniture to fill up the new house. A bed settee from the old flat. Tw rickety bookcases. A coffee table from Paul's mam's house. Boxes and boxes of yellowing paperbacks. Half of the books Paul has heaped up, waiting to be read, he takes out there and piles up to the ceiling of the Beach House. On the walls they hang paintings in frames they have picked up at car-boot sales and charity shops. All of them are ocean scenes or pictures of beaches. Shells and driftwood and large pebbles from days out by the seaside find their places on the shelves.

But best of all is the butterfly chair, which goes against the far window, where the afternoon light comes streaming through. It's wickerwork, with a cushion that I've already covered in hair. There is no doubt that this is meant to be Fester's chair.

And so it becomes my favourite perch in the whole garden.

Paul lies down on the bed settee. He's got a whole bunch of throws and cushions on there already. He's got a stack of murder mysteries, paranormal romances, and science-fiction novels on the coffee table. He's got a basket of vintage comics and magazines, and a heap of notebooks and all kinds of pens.

Jeremy's on the veranda, on a wooden

chair, with a huge mug of tea, surveying his garden.

The wood pigeons hoot. Ziggy howls next door. There's all that revving of motorbike engines. Trains rumble by into Piccadilly.

But this is the most peaceful I think we've ever been.

This is it. We keep quite still and quiet and content. We all know it. We've all three gone and found our perfect place in the world.

OUT OF THE MAINSTREAM

Out here Paul writes more of his spooky adventures for the ladies of Whitby. He drinks an amazing number of cups of tea and coffee. He starts his blog and has endless fun with that, writing about books and days out and all about me. Me and him in the Beach House. He posts many, many pictures of me sitting with him, sitting with teacups and paperbacks and friends of his. He writes all day long while his laptop battery runs down, and when it's gone he scribbles in notebooks. He makes up stories for *Doctor Who* and other travelers in time and space. He thinks about new stories he might get into. About how stories work. About how one universe links into another. He thinks too much, probably. But at least he's out in the fresh air.

Messages from the world outside seem to matter less and less.

"You're so hard to sell, you see. You're

hard to pin down and put a label on. Your books look like one thing, and then they turn into another. They're irreverent. They don't play the genre game by the rules. They have as their characters old ladies and gay men. They're ironic, they're whimsical, they're occasionally silly. You aren't mainstream enough. Can't you be a bit more conventional? You're such a hard sell. You're such a hard fit. You won't 'break through.' There isn't a mass market for stuff like this. It's too difficult to explain to the sales and marketing team. Can't you make it simpler? Can't you make it more straightforward? What about having younger protagonists? What about more guns? What about not writing about the north anymore and writing about middle-class people in the south? What about making it darker, edgier? What about cutting out all the daft jokes and ironic bits? What about just playing the game and behaving well? What about learning to toe the line? Can't you do that? Can't you? Can't you just go with the flow? Can't you fit in? Can't you stay on-message? Can't you just be the same as everyone else?"

No thanks, Paul thinks.

And I think the same.

No, we bloomin' well can't.

SMOKEY

One day we're sitting on the patio at the back and there comes the most horrible noise. It's an unearthly noise. A screeching noise. It's like something being put to death. All three of us sit up straight in alarm. Hairs go up on the back of our necks.

The screeches are cruelly prolonged, and they're joined by a barrage of gruff barking. We all know at once it's the sound of a dog getting hold of a cat. A dog getting hold and not letting go.

Jeremy and Paul are on their feet at once. Jeremy goes running into the alleyway. Paul heads that way too, then he turns and picks me up because he's worried I'll go running towards the source of the sound. But I wouldn't. I lie in his arms, transfixed by the noise.

I notice Three-Legged Freddie, shrinking into the undergrowth.

Who is it? Who's been caught?

There are more screams, more barking. Then there are human shouts. Men bellowing at each other. A younger man's voice. They get louder and louder — and then suddenly fade. It all goes very quiet. Ominously quiet.

After a few minutes Jeremy comes back.

"It's Smokey," he says. He looks very grim.

I struggle in Paul's arms. I don't know what I'm trying to do. I don't know what I can do to help.

"What's happened?" asks Paul.

"There were two lads with an Alsatian. They came under the railway tunnel and they didn't have it on the lead. It came running down Berkley Avenue, and turned the corner. And then it saw Smokey there, sitting in his usual place."

Straightaway I can see it. The dog running way ahead of its owners. Just two lads. Too far away for them to catch up.

And then I can see Smokey. Sitting on his heap of mud. Or in the hollow by the trees he favours. Or on that low wall in front of his house towards the end of Chestnut Avenue. He'd have been sitting there. A great big mound of fur. Black and white, fading to grey. The granddaddy of all the cats round here. Minding his own business. Blinking in the sun. Half blind. Half lame.

Not even knowing what hit him.

"What happened?" Paul asks again.

"The dog saw Smokey and just went for him. There was a struggle . . . not much of one. Smokey's owners soon heard the noise, and hurried to their front door. Smokey got away, and went running into the house, as fast as he could. Now he's down in their cellar. He's hiding as far away as he can get. They can't even get to him to have a look at him. They don't know how badly hurt he is . . ."

"Where's the dog?"

"The lads managed to get it away. They went running off, though . . ."

We all sit there in shock.

How can anything happen to Smokey? He's the oldest cat on the block. He's like a monument. He's stately, elderly. No one even knows how old he is. The idea of him running for his life. Of his being grabbed up in the slavering jaws of some crazed dog. Of him struggling and bleeding — and then limping away into a dark corner of the cellar . . .

It's knocked me sick. I want to go to him. I want to go and see if we can talk him out. He must come out. He could be down there lying in the earthy dark of the cellar, bleeding to death.

But I can't make the boys understand. How can I tell them? How can I make them understand that maybe I can help? I've known Smokey since forever. Since I was little, even.

For as long as I remember.

If anything happens, then I'll be the oldest cat on Chestnut Avenue. I don't think I'm ready for that.

Come on, Smokey. Pull through.

Later that day, Jeremy goes round the house where Smokey has lived all his life. It's a minister and his wife who live there. Jeremy and Paul know them enough to say hello to. When he goes round Jeremy learns that one of the boys with the Alsatian returned a little later. Just when everyone was calling him worse than muck. When everyone was lamenting the shameless, savage youth of today, this lad came back to ask them how the cat was. He came back in tears. He was distraught. He was terrified their cat had been killed and that he'd have to have his dog destroyed.

It was an upsetting afternoon all round.

We sat outside as the daylight faded. The screeching and barking still rang in our ears. We waited for news of Smokey.

When it came at last it was encouraging. They had calmed Smokey slightly. He was

still shaking, though, when they managed to draw him out of the darkness. He crept into their arms and he lay nerveless and bleeding in their arms.

They rushed him to the emergency vet and had him stitched and sorted out.

He had survived. He was alive. It looked like he might come through.

That night I jump onto the bed with Paul as he reads, and we wait together for Jeremy to come to bed. The windows are open on the cooling breeze that wafts through the back gardens. Paul knows I need soothing. I've had — we've all had — a horrible reminder about the dangers out there. The hideous, everyday dangers of being this small. We're just scraps of bloomin' flesh, aren't we? Little bits of bone. Easy prey to other, bigger animals.

I try hard to calm down. To draw deep breaths. To sleep easily.

Smokey stays home for a good long while.

Weeks and months go by and word has it that he's an indoor cat now. His courage is shattered. His nerve has gone. And no wonder, I think. We'll never see him again sitting outside his house, watching all the world. I feel like I'm never going to see him again.

Months go by. Months and months.

Now I'm a bit nervous going out the front. I watch warily from the doorstep when Paul goes to the door. I imagine how Smokey must have felt, suddenly caught up in those jaws.

And then, much later, when we think Smokey has vanished from public life forever, he surprises us all.

He's walking up Chestnut Avenue, easy as you please. Looking quite different. Looking ten years younger.

We all stare in astonishment as Smokey saunters past our front garden.

He's been shaved. I guess they had to do that because of the stitches he had.

But even all these months later, he's kept the look. And now he's the skinniest, slinkiest cat I've ever seen. Pale grey and felty. Though his head hasn't been shaved at all. He looks like he's wearing his own face as a carnival mask. And his tail is still thick and feathery. He has little bootees of fur. But the rest of him is strangely svelte. We all have to blink several times when we see him go by.

"Smokey!" I call out. "It's me!"

He shouts back gruffly and gives a little skip. "Hello there, Fester!"

"Look at you! You look so well!"

"I feel rather marvellous, as it happens,"

he says. "I've lost a tonne of weight!"

"Hurray for you, Smokey! Ungow!"

"Ungow, Fester!" he cries.

We see him again once or twice after that. His courage has come back, and he's still looking great. But soon it's time for him to stay indoors and live a much quieter life. And not long after that, we don't hear anything about Smokey anymore.

In Paris

I'm glad they get away for a while. The two of them go off flying again in August and I think they can both do with some time away from their desks. When they talk about flying I still can't shake the idea of them simply going off and taking to the skies. All those heavy bags they pack — bright orange and sea green — try to weigh them down, but the two of them simply go zooming off and soaring into the skies above South Manchester like the pigeons do.

They leave early in the morning, talking excitedly about being on the Left Bank in Paris by lunchtime. Yeah, yeah, I tell them, as if it's all a big pretend. Well, you two enjoy it. You deserve a rest.

I watch from the front window as the taxi comes and carries them away, and I realise I've a few days on my own with Radio 3 and 4.

It's late in the summer and I suppose that

means it's coming up to an anniversary for us. Wasn't it a September when I moved in? I don't even know how many years ago that was. It seems like lots and lots. Like I've said, cats don't measure time like humans do. We stand on its surface, or we stand inside it. I'm not even sure where we stand, but we feel it differently. The years go by and they chime against each other, they echo and we feel the changes differently from how humans do. In this summer I feel the echoes and changes of many different summers. I feel like the best ones are the most recent. The ones in the late summer of my whole life.

I've three or four days to muse on that in the dusky house. The long velvet curtains are pulled against the too-hot sun. I lie on my pink throw. It's sumptuous with cat hair and grayish dirt.

They're doing their favourite holiday, as I close my eyes and drowse through these days. They repeat the same holiday almost every year, when they can afford to. They visit the same cafés and restaurants. They sit under the leafy boughs of Notre-Dame and in the shaded nooks of the Latin Quarter. They visit the same galleries and see Matisse and Picasso in the Marais, mummi-ed cats in the Louvre and Toulouse-

Lautrec in the Musée d'Orsay. They walk along the riverbank mooching by bookstalls and sitting on benches eating pastries and fruit. When I picture them they're just gliding about in the streets of mostly shuttered shops and apartment buildings. Paris is closed down for the summer, but this is how they like it. Wandering in the grey streets through the brown dust of summer under yellow sunlight in shorts, flip-flops, and linen shirts.

I approve of everything they do because it's become so catlike. Paul is happy sitting for hours in a green chair in the park, hidden between the tall trees of the Jardin du Luxembourg. He's got a pile of paperbacks from the San Francisco bookshop and he's kicked off his trainers and it's like the whole of Paris has become his back garden.

Jeremy's going round statues and fountains, taking photos, snapping strange, oblique viewpoints and close-ups. He loves bright, colourful pictures of blistered paint on doors, and dark, interesting windows.

They squabble and chat and go for contented hours without talking. Sometimes they fight and fume at each other for ages. Some days Paul would be happy staying still in the Tuileries, having ice cream and café crèmes under a café awning, and Jerem wants to go walking. They end up walking much too far, looping the loop round the city streets, and by evening they're parched and exhausted. But all the while they're excited. Even when they're fighting or bored or making each other miserable or laughing like drains. They're still in Paris. They're still having fun. They're still making everything up as they go along.

Hours spent sitting on top of the Arabian Institute, in the rooftop café with mint tea and baklava. Hours in the Natural History Museum, paying attention to the parade of stuffed animals and the hall of extinct beasts. Hours walking to and from the contemporary art institute, having lunch in a graffitied palace overrun by daredevil skater boys. In the Museum of Modern Art they see Paul's favourite-ever painting in the flesh, quite by accident: a pink room painted by Raoul Dufy. The most perfect, glamorous room in the world.

But I know they're missing me. Later, they tell me that the dark, narrow staircase going up to their hotel room smelled very strongly of cat wee. Decades' worth of ineradicable feline piddle. I felt very proud when they told me it reminded them of me, and made them homesick. Even so, they made sure they relished every moment of their being away.

Each evening finished in a bar on top of a boat moored near Notre-Dame, where they toasted each other, Panda, and me in cloudy pastis. The cathedral loomed pale grey and ghostly over the Seine. Its gargoyles leering down at the passing pleasure boats. The kind of place, Paul said, nearly every time they were there, that made you shiver from sheer pleasure at the thought of simply being there. I can't believe I'm actually here, he thought, every time he was in Paris.

Jeremy — dafty that he is — took his laptop with him.

For most of their long weekend he resisted opening it up and connecting. Then, just before breakfast on the third day, he brought it downstairs and connected up to the Wi-Fi. He had several dozen work e-mails that had reached him over the weekend. Most of them were from the boss who seemed intent on making his life so difficult. They began quite reasonably, but as the weekend went by, they had become more and more complicated and odd. By Monday breakfast he was demanding immediate attention.

"Has something gone wrong?" Paul asked, concerned.

They were at a table by the window. Croissants and crusty bread had arrived. Yoghurt and honey were set down before them with the most perfect, dark coffee. Jeremy was ignoring Paul's questions, sipping his coffee, crumbling a pastry, and trying to take in what his e-mails were saying. The laptop was like a third person at the table with them. It never left his knee. Jeremy was trying to reply to things as he ate. He was red and quiet and intent.

"Is there an emergency?" Paul asked.

"Just the usual stuff," was all Jeremy said. He didn't want to explain more.

"But do you need to do it at breakfast?" Paul asked. "I mean, you're on holiday. He knows you're away. Surely it can wait? Surely you can deal with it when we get back . . ."

"It's about the conference next month," Jeremy said. "And the Annual General Meeting and getting all the papers sorted for that."

"But you're on holiday."

"I know."

"Well, you can't do it now."

But Jeremy kept on replying to e-mails. He pushed aside his breakfast things, and set about replying to the e-mails in earnest. "Look, if I just do this now. These few things he's after . . . then maybe he'll leave me alone . . ."

But Jeremy had been up till two in the morning doing similar stuff, the very night before they'd left on holiday, and every night for weeks before. He was like an addict, the way he talked about responding to the requests of this man who was his boss. Paul wasn't happy, but he couldn't stop him. Jeremy wouldn't listen. This bloke wasn't going away.

Somehow that day never quite came together after that. Even though all the e-mails were done in less than an hour, and Jeremy felt he had staved off his boss at least for a few hours more, there was a gap between the two of them. Paul was angry, and knew he shouldn't be. It was hardly Jeremy's fault.

They walked about Saint-Germain, and there was a sudden downpour. They sheltered in Café de Flore, ordering thick, creamy hot chocolate, which was served from scalding silver pots into white bone china.

"That bloke is always having a go at you," Paul said.

"I don't want to talk about it now," Jeremy said.

THE POND

It's the summer when Jeremy builds his pond in the garden. That's when it happens to me.

There's a hollow in the middle of the garden where there used to be a huge tree. I actually remember it being there, that's the funny thing. When this was just another garden that I'd visit, in the years when I was a stray. It was the biggest tree in the whole street, and it was lousy with squirrels and magpies. It was here, they said, even before they built Chestnut Avenue itself, when this was a farm.

But the tree got too big and its roots were growing too close to the house. It was the last lot of owners of our house who had it chopped down and taken away. Like everything they did, they made a mess of the job — Jeremy tells us crossly. He's already furious with them a dozen times over for the jobs they botched and the corners they cut with DIY in the house. And when they chopped down the tree they left solid hardwood roots stuck in the earth. He tries to dig them out, and to burn them, but there seems no way of getting rid of them.

But the middle bit of the garden wants to be a pond. When there's heavy rain it fills up with tea-coloured water. In the spring we get frogs coming out of nowhere, heading busily towards the makeshift pool. They're looking for somewhere to settle.

Eventually Jeremy starts building a pond, doing it just the way his dad did in his garden in Perth. He digs down and down, and lines the square hole with heavy black plastic. He works for what seems like weeks on building the pond. I keep inspecting the work through the long, warm days, and toddle down to the Beach House to fill Paul in on progress.

Paul's spending that summer immersed in several big projects. Two novels, he reckons, and a number of scripts for *Doctor Who*. "The telly?" I gasp. But he reckons they're just audiobooks, but I'm still pleased for him. Every couple of weeks he goes to London and has a day or two in a studio with people there. Cast members and a lively crew of coworkers who are all involved in making these CDs of *Doctor Who* adventures. He seems to have a wonderful time. He can't believe he's actually spending time with Doctor Who. With Tom Baker, his favourite Doctor Who.

When he puts aside his laptop and lies down on the bed settee, I dash into the Beach House and sit on his chest. "Ungow," I tell him.

We both listen to the thunderous roar of the pond filling up. It's the big day when Jeremy's decided the pond is ready for it, and he's left the hose pipe dangling into the great dark hole. The noise is deep and gurgling, and could send you off to sleep.

Both Paul and I think that the pond might be a bit too big. It's at least three times the size and depth we expected.

"But just imagine when it's done," Jeremy has said. "There'll be a little wooden platform all around it for Fester to walk on, and there'll be lily pads floating on the top, and rushes and huge-leafed plants surrounding it. We'll have a little bank of grass sloping down from its edge, and you can lie there and read, with Fester next to you, when the sun's right over that part of the garden."

"Will there be fish?" I ask him pointedly.

It turns out that a pond is something you have to develop gradually. It grows and matures with the seasons. At the moment it just looks like a huge bath of tap water, but soon enough, it will be deep and gloomy and mysterious. It will also be teeming with all kinds of life.

Our garden has become a wonderful world, all of its own. Jeremy has enclosed it with tall plants and bushes. It's become like a secret garden, hidden away from the rest of the street.

Some days that summer are barbecue days, and the boys invite neighbours and friends around. These can be rather drunken do's, with lots of laughing and messing about. I hang about on the patio, quite enjoying tidbits from the charcoal griddle, and hanging about with familiar faces. These are long days, lasting until after the sun's gone down, and the cat parade has been and gone. These are great days.

But it's the middle of that summer when something happens to me.

I don't even recognise what it is at first. I just feel different. Warmer. Mithered. My fur gets a bit matted down my back, because I'm sweating hard. A bit too feverish. I think I've probably sat too long in the sun. I've fallen asleep on my plank. I've lain in the full sunlight on the middle of the lawn, and the brightness has given me a headache.

Then I realise what the strange thing is. I'm off my food.

They notice quickly. They watch me stick my nose into my dish of cat food in the mornings, and then turn away sadly. Don't fancy that much. Maybe later. That makes me feel a bit sickly. I'm queasy in the mornings. What's that about? Not even switching flavours helps. Switching from meaty to fishy pouches. That particular Monday, Tuesday, Wednesday, nothing can tempt me.

I'm as puzzled as the boys are.

"We all have off days," Jeremy says. "Just leave him be. He'll come and eat when he's ready."

The days are too bright to go out in. I sit indoors, even when all the doors are open and the garden's at its most inviting. I don't even fancy going out to see the pond when it's completely full and the boys are calling.

What I do instead is creep about the house, very carefully. Feeling sore and slightly cross. Nothing against the boys. They're just concerned. But I don't want fussing and I don't want to bother them. I find a corner where I don't think they'll come looking for me. I have a look in Jeremy's hugely messy study and I squeeze myself behind a chest of drawers. There's a very dusty canyon between the chest and

271

the wall. Just enough for me to lie in. That's where I'll stay for a while. It's cool and dry and I just need to keep still for a time. That's all.

Of course, it's not long before they come and find me.

But I'm glad, really. Because even lying here in quiet, I'm not feeling any better. Paul lifts me out. He's read somewhere that cats hide themselves away when they're ill. He wants to know what's wrong with me.

I try to behave as normal. I try to eat. I throw it back up on a rug upstairs.

That night Jeremy decides, "We'll see how he is in the morning, and if he's no better we'll take him to the hairdresser's."

That night I lie on the landing, watching for monsters. But my mind isn't really on it. I'm trying to feel hungry. I'm trying to feel normal.

In the middle of the night I walk around their bed and hop onto Paul's side and go and lie near his pillows. There's a space for me to lie right next to his face.

His breathing helps me to sleep.

But in the morning I have to admit. I feel worse.

Jeremy is full of action. He goes down to their messy, overfull cellar and brings out the Selfridges carry case, which I haven' seen since my operation on my teeth and gums. When was that? Ages ago. Years ago? I don't even know. It's been so long since I had to go to the hairdresser's and be treated with kid gloves and looked after like that. I've been so strong and well. And now this. I feel weak and sickly, and when I even look at my feeding station all my insides feel funny.

They make an appointment for that very morning and carry me out to the car. Paul sits with me on his lap as we drive through the backstreets and I can feel the worry coming out of him in waves. And I know he doesn't want it to, in case he worries me. But I'm already worried. I don't know why I feel like this. Or maybe I do. Maybe this is it. This is the end.

THE HAIRDRESSER'S

Mr Joe feels all down my sides with both hands. He looks like he's listening to what his fingers are telling him. But I don't feel any sharp pain. Nothing to make me cry out. He's quite firm, pushing his fingers into my fur. "He's lost a bit of weight," my hairdresser muses.

Both boys are standing by the examination table, quietly and still.

It's decided that a blood sample is needed. That's okay. That's no big deal. I've had that before. I'm not worried about that.

I've got an infection, so I get a jab for that, and a course of pills.

Mr. Joe says come back at teatime that same day, to find out about my blood.

We drive home again and my head is swimming with antibiotics and the medicine feels cold on my empty stomach.

I'm so glad to see home again. The blue gravel and the pink-painted front doo

When the door is open it's a clear path down the wooden floor all the way to the back door. When that's open and you can see all the green of the overgrown bushes and trees, it's like the whole house is just a tunnel leading to our secret garden.

There's a long afternoon of waiting to come before we return to the hairdresser's. I know where I want to be. Under the canopy of leaves, under the cool roof of the Beach House. I curl up on the bed settee with Paul. I lie in the crook of his legs as he reads, and he talks to me a bit, as if he can take both our minds off the blood test. But neither of us forgets, of course. We know we're going back there. At least, I think we are. Is that how I'm feeling? Or do I think that's it and that's all the treatment done with? Do I think I'm all better now and on the mend? I don't know. I feel preoccupied. I feel like I'm listening for something. Waiting for something. But I don't know what.

And then I realise. I haven't gone home with them.

I'm not sitting in Fester's Beach House after all.

That's all in my head.

What I'm doing is sitting in one of these cages at the back of the vet's on the Stockport Road. The white blinds are pulled against the sun and I can hear the traffic noise swelling. Other cages hold sick cats and dogs and there are whimpers and mews, and deep, sleepy breaths.

They've left me here. Mr. Joe told them I'd be better off here while my bloods were sent off to the lab, to be looked at and analysed. I know the boys wanted to take me home. I know they'd rather have me with them. Then we could have waited together. All together as we always are. But Mr. Joe said it was best if I spent the afternoon here with the other sick animals.

So I had that little dream as the medicine swirled through my body. They tried to get me to eat and drink just a little bit. I tried my best and went into my dream. A small dream of going home to our garden.

I hope it won't be too much longer before I see it again. For real.

But I just don't know. How could I know?

I just have to wait. I know they'll come back. Whatever the outcome. Whatever my blood tells them is wrong with me. I know I'm at least going to see the boys again.

Even if it's just one more time.

LONG AFTERNOON

It's the longest afternoon in the world.

At home Paul sits in Fester's House, and Jeremy returns to work at his computer. He's still getting those very troublesome messages from his boss. Sometimes the man phones up to harangue him, or gets other people in the organisation to have a go. Jeremy is feeling alone with this stuff. He starts to panic, sitting at his desk, staring at the wide computer screen. He's tried explaining it all to Paul. Paul tries to understand but he gets so caught up in his own work and his own tussles. Paul's head is full of books and Jeremy can't always get through to him.

As the afternoon goes on Paul finds he can't escape into books as much as he'd like. It seems he needs a certain familiar presence there with him in order to do so. None of the stories make sense. All the words seem absurd. Everything he reads becomes pointless and worthless, the second he tries to read it. His own work is worse. He makes the mistake of attempting to distract himself by reading over drafts and notes of what he's working on. All at once it seems stupid. Useless.

His attention keeps getting snagged by the fact that there's no one climbing onto his knee and settling there and staring up at him. He keeps glancing down at the rug, expecting to see Fester sitting at cat attention, his chest puffed out and his feet neatly together. Waiting to be asked to jump up. There's no one sprawled on the veranda of the Beach House as the sunlight smoothes its way tenderly over the pale wood, trickling through the dense magnolia leaves.

The furry cushion on the bamboo chair is empty. There's a hollow in it. It's only recently been vacated.

Paul puts all his imagination not into reading or writing, but into trying to picture my not coming back. He twists the thought through his mind. He even starts crying, the daft sod. I know he's doing it to prepare himself — if the worst comes to the worst. Torturing himself with superstition like humans often do. But what he needs to know is that it isn't over yet. While he's trying to fathom a life without me, at that very moment I'm plying all my own energy into making sure I keep myself alive.

Diagnosis

I think all of us feel like it's one of those days that will never end.

The boys are due back at the hairdresser's at 6:15. Time drags for all of us. Me most of all, I think. I go into a kind of trance, blocking out the cage and the noises around me. Sitting patiently, biding my time. Trusting things are going to get better than this.

I must remember this feeling on other days. When days slip by so easily. When days are so easy to waste. When they gallop by and it seems so luxurious, napping between lunch and dinner and supper. When there's nothing particularly pressing on my attention. If I'm lucky enough to have free and simple days like that again, I must remember what it was like to be on this timetable. To feel fenced in by time, and not to know what was going to become of me. I must never forget this, I think as I curl up in the airport blanket from home and lick my paws, which smell comfortingly of homely dirt.

Then sometime after six o'clock the nurse comes in and tells me that my fellas are here, and that Mr. Joe is back from his break, and has been sent an e-mail by the laboratory in Stockport, where they were paying close attention to my blood sample. She hoicks me out of my cell and carries me back to Mr. Joe's surgery. I'm limp with excitement and terror.

Mr. Joe is talking to Paul and Jeremy when I am brought in. He's holding a piece of paper covered in tiny print and numbers and explaining things to them. They all look to see me arrive in the room, and as the nurse puts me gently on the padded table.

"Here he is," she says, and Jeremy reaches out to touch my ears and to tickle under my chin. The nurse says something about me being such a calm and well-behaved boy.

I look at both Paul and Jeremy, drinking them in. Seeing as much as I can of them all at once. Taking them in like years have gone by since I saw them last. They're so familiar. The smell of them. The scent of home. They're towering presences. They both scratch my chin and I know both are itching to pick me up. But Mr. Joe is talking and explaining, and they both must be good

281

boys too, and listen to what he says.

He holds a long list of things they found in my blood. Numbers tell him all about what my blood is made of. What's in it and what's not in it. What's chugging around my system.

As Paul listens to all the details he's looking at me, and thinking I look so tiny. In this context, away from home, I look and feel really small. And the list they're hearing is all about microscopic stuff. Details to do with things we can't even see. The details of huge, dramatic stuff going on inside me right now. All at once I feel pretty important.

Mr. Joe is telling them that it can be plainly inferred from the results he's been sent that my problem lies with my thyroid. It is hyperactive.

Both boys wait for more details. They're anguished and still, needing to be told more.

"In a cat of this age, you'd expect liver or kidney or problems with his heart, but they are fine. His kidneys aren't great, but they're okay. But what this is clearly telling us, if you look here . . ."

Blah, blah. He says a whole load of stuff that's a bit too technical for me. All I'm thinking about is the stuff swimming through my system. All these chemicals and things with funny names. Who'd have thought I was as complex as this?

"The main thing," says Mr. Joe, "is that it's treatable."

The boys both let out a huge sigh of relief.

"It's treatable with a daily tablet, for the rest of his life. You can pick up a month's supply at a time from here. Just phone the day before you need them each month, and we'll get them in ready for him."

Mr. Joe tickles me under the chin, just missing my Special Spot above my collarbone. Oddly enough, that's just about where he said this thyroid gland actually lies. Just a tiny little thing. It's working a bit wrongly. It's been affecting my whole metabolism for quite some time.

I love the thought of my having such a thing as a metabolism. And here's all these human beings paying it such serious attention!

I'll need to go back for checks and blood tests in the future. They will want to keep tabs on me. But that's all right. I can cope with that. And we can cope with a tablet a day, can't we, boys?

I look up again at them, and at Mr. Joe.

"Well then," he says. "So you can go home."

I can hardly believe my luck.

My heart is hammering with joy as they

pop me back into my carry case.

They take me to reception, where strangers are sitting with their own carry cases, looking worried and scared. I want to say: Don't worry so much. It might be all right. They will do their best for you. You too could be going home again. Home again like Fester Cat!

They set me on the counter and pay the bill and receive their first month's supply of tiny pink pills. They come in such a small brown bottle, scrunched into a paper bag.

While this is going on Paul's pushing his face up to the front of my carry case and talking to me. He's whispering the Fester Cat song to me, to make me feel all right and to reassure me.

But I feel fantastic.

I mean, I still feel a bit sickly as a result of the infection I picked up when I was so run-down. And underneath that I feel absolutely starved. I've gone wretched and skinny because of this illness. And now I know that's all to do with my metabolism.

But I know that I'm going to get better.

They've got my tablets.

Take me home, boys. Load me into the Škoda. Just a few streets away, through the zigzagging roads of Levenshulme, and we're heading back home. Back from the hairdresser's again! Back home in triumph once more!

As we drive and I sit on Paul's knee in the case that came from Selfridges, they both sing the song to me. They sing it at the top of their voices and throw in several "Ungows!" for good measure.

And before we even know it, we're home.

And the last of the long day's sun is still slanting across our garden. We're home in time to stay outside, having a nice sit-down.

TAKING THE MEDICINE

We keep my tablets in a small ceramic box. It's brightly painted, with a lion's face on the lid. It was one of a bunch of souvenirs the boys brought back from Paris last time they went. At the time it had no real function, like many of the bits that clutter up their shelves. But now it's the place where Fester's tablets are kept.

I take one every morning, first thing, before breakfast. We've had some elaborate fun and games getting into this routine.

I really don't like the taste of these pink pills. They're dry and quite nasty. I can't take them crushed up into my food, either, because they make the food taste horrible, and I can detect them from a mile off. They can't fool me.

There's a certain technique they've read about in a book about caring for cats. It involves taking a firm hand and holding your cat against your body like a set of bagpipes, and squeezing open the poor thing's jaws. Then you pop the pill easily into the open mouth, and the cat swallows it down. So says the book. Well, that ended up in a few nasty scenes. I wriggled and scratched and lashed out and hissed. I shouted at them both to cease and desist. I couldn't quite believe that having read some duff advice in some silly book, the two of them thought they could get the knack of such rough carryings-on.

The first week following my medical emergency is worst, because I'm on daily antibiotic pills too, and they taste even worse than my thyroid tablets.

I become very adept at spitting the foul things out.

Pfffft. Pfffft.

Pills fly through the air. They shoot across the kitchen floor, bouncing off the wooden boards — *click click click* — and lodging finally inside impossible crevices.

Pfffft.

Then the boys remember the trick they used a little while ago, when I was last on a course of pills for worms. They take the thyroid tablets and coat them one at a time in chicken liver pâté.

Instant result.

Their faces light up in delight.

Crunch crunch crunch.

It's gone in an instant. Crunched between my one and a half teeth and swallowed up with relish. I'd do anything at all for chicken liver pâté. For Ardennes pâté. For Brussels pâté. For mackerel pâté. We rotate different kinds to keep my morning taste buds intrigued, and there's always an open tub of the heavenly stuff with my name on it in the fridge.

So we settle into a routine with my medication. Every month the boys order a new little bottle. Every morning I come bunny-hopping down the stairs with Paul, hurrying to the door when he brings in the milk. And I know that the first thing I have to do, before I can get any pouch food, is swallow down some pâté. A wodge of chicken liver containing a hard and pink little biscuit.

Paul says I should think of it as a canapé. An appetizer. And so that's what I do.

And I lick all the pâté off the ends of his fingers, once I've taken the pill. Sometimes I struggle. It drops out of my mouth because I can't get it right between my teeth. Sometimes Paul has to try again and again, picking the tablet up and coating it in pâté again. And sometimes that's because I can't quite manage to catch hold of it, or because I can't stomach it just yet. Other times it's simply because I want another helping of pâté.

But all my days begin with this task — this tiny thing that I know, deep down, is keeping this little cat alive. And really, on the best of days, it's a luxurious treat. That's the way we've all decided to think about it.

Changes Round Our Way

I don't know where Three-Legged Freddie went to.

We were so used to seeing him in the alleyway, and in the road, holding up the traffic as he went round and round, his back legs dragging in the dirt, and all his fur hanging down. Then, after a while, we realised we hadn't seen him much at all. Likewise Whisper, the mardy Siamese.

Things were changing round our street. The old dark house that burned down that time. Someone had done it all up, brand spanking new. Then there was a shifting population coming through because it had been changed into flats. There was an old man who would sit with his legs dangling out of his second-storey window, gargling his own phlegm and spitting it into the trees. Jeremy got so fed up he shouted at him and told him to get himself back indoors.

There were other barbecues, other lazy Sunday afternoons, and other rainy autumn mornings, when the kids went back to school and Paul went back to the university term. He read huge piles of student novels and I sat with him as he ploughed his way through. The neighbours from the end house adopted two children, a little blond boy and girl. And so we met them, and they were very interested in meeting me — and Panda.

Paul and some of the neighbours started up a Book Club, and met once a month round each other's houses. The first was in our kitchen, and I sat at the pine table with them, with their wine and snacks. "Getting Drunk and Gossiping Club" was what Jeremy called it, because he reckoned they didn't talk about the books much. Caroline and Karen came round, and then Jamie joined for a while. I learned that Jamie worked at the radio station where Smooth Seventies came from. That was pretty impressive. He was pleased to hear about Cat Discos at Lunchtime in our kitchen. Mostly, though, he came round to watch *Doctor Who,* which he loved as much as the boys did. I curled on his knee and listened to him talk about his cat, Ben.

Still Jeremy was worried about his work.

He let it take over everything. He kept us all awake at night by refusing to go to bed and getting stressed over his computer and all the messages coming through. He faced an impossible mountain of work. His boss kept saying that he had to catch up. He had to get everything done. And whenever Jeremy thought he was making progress the boss would start shouting about something, some tiny thing that wasn't right.

Jeremy was getting moodier and angrier. He was losing his temper more often. He would smash things up. Paul would cook meals and he wouldn't come down for them. He would stay in his room and the cigarette smoke would come drifting down to fill the whole house.

WALKING OUT

Paul's on his phone in the Beach House.

I'm on his knee, now that he's put his laptop down.

Today's twelve hundred words are done and I'm sitting there getting a pat while he talks to Jasmine.

He's upset. I can hear it in his voice. I don't know what it's about exactly. But he's cross and just about crying.

I've been asleep most of the morning. It's warm and gorgeous. I've been on my wickerwork chair. Maybe Jeremy and Paul have had words yet again? Maybe I've missed an argument.

I try to pick up on what he's saying. I recognise Jasmine's voice at the other end. Distant and tinny.

"Well, why don't you?" she says.

"I suppose I could . . ." He frowns. He tickles my chin and I rub my whole jaw vigorously against his knuckles. I get sleep drool all over his hand, but he doesn't mind. Come on, now, I think. Rub my eyebrows. My whiskers. My bloomin' moustache. Do mammy cat ears!

He ruffles my ears wonderfully and so I don't hear much more of the conversation until he reaches the point where he's made a decision. "Yeah, you're right. I just need to get out. I need to get away for a bit. Give myself some clear space to think. I need to see how I feel when I'm away from here. When I'm not surrounded by all the mess and I'm not stuck with those bloody moods of his . . ."

"Ungow?"

Is he going away?

"Are you sure that's okay, though?" he asks Jasmine.

I hear her witter on some more, at the other end. But I don't quite get the gist. She talks to Paul like she does me, as if we're slightly daft.

"It would be a huge help," he's saying now. "If I could just come and stay for a couple of days. It would be brilliant. And we could have a day out or something, couldn't we? We never get to spend any time together. I'll cook you dinner! And it might do Jeremy good, to be here just getting on with work, without me here . . ."

Now, I don't like the sound of this at all.

Paul is making plans now. Jasmine will meet him at a train station near hers. He's going to check out times and text her. He's full of busy, all of a sudden. Does this mean he's going to leave now?

"Okay," he says. "I'm going to do it. I'll see you by lunchtime. I'll pack some things and just go."

My heart starts pounding.

He finishes his call, puts me down on the ground, and picks up his laptop and all his stuff from the Beach House. He asks me, "Are you staying out here, Fester Cat, or are you coming back inside?"

I follow him down the garden, down my plank, across the patio. I follow him into the house. I don't even pause by my smorgasbord for a snack. I don't want to let him out of my sight.

We go upstairs. Jeremy's talking loudly on the phone. We can hear him through his closed door.

Paul goes to the bedroom and pulls his going-away bag down from the wardrobe. He throws it onto the bed, which is still rumpled and full of sun from this morning.

I jump up too, and paw at the handles.

"Come out of the way, Fester." He's concentrating on unfolding clothes and dragging clean shirts from hangers. Suddenly he's as locked into himself as Jeremy is. He almost seems angry.

I shove my whole head into his going-away bag, sniffing into the dark corners.

"You can't come away with me, Fester," he says. "Come on. Let me pack."

"Ungow?"

I back off and move away. I curl up on the blue blanky, watching him hard. Every move he makes. I watch the clothes he's taking away. How many days' worth? I can't work it out. He's taking my favourite jumper of his. And the softest blue shirt.

He kisses me on the top of my head and leaves me sitting on the middle stair. He calls out from the front door to Jeremy. "I'm going."

Jeremy doesn't realise until a few minutes after the front door's banged shut behind him. "Where's he gone, Fester?"

"Mow," I say, because I can't summon up a whole "Ungow."

Jeremy thunders down the stairs and into the kitchen. I follow, and he's putting the kettle on, then texting Paul. Jeremy has about a hundred cups of tea a day. Each one in the biggest mug he can find, milky and strong. He pours out a tiny bit of milk into one of my fancy blue dishes, which I push my nose into briefly. I only lap a little up because I've been told it's not actually all that good for me. I stand on the kitchen table and stare at Jeremy. I try to get through to him.

"Paul's gone off. He doesn't know when he's going to be back."

Paul doesn't reply to Jeremy's texts for a little while. Not while he's at Piccadilly and waiting for the tram to Jasmine's house in North Manchester. We both imagine him on the platform under the ground, out of texting range while he's trying to figure out the map of the tram lines and the departure times. His hastily packed bag of crumpled clothes on the ground.

I haven't been to Jasmine's house, of course. So my imagination runs out about here. I've only ever seen her when she's been at our house, all clunky beads and jewellery, wearing shawls and lumpy clothes. I can't picture her house, where Paul is going rather than staying here with us. I imagine it being like a nest, perhaps. Or like the squirrels' drey at the top of our beech tree. A bit messy with twigs sticking out on the outside, but incredibly tidy inside. Very organised. Almost too tidy.

"He won't be gone for long, Fester," Jeremy says. He drinks his tea at the kitchen sink. He looks red-faced and tired. He needs to come and sit in the sun and air. I hop off the table and pad to the back door. Come out here. Come and look at your plants. Come and see the quince tree, the cherry tree, the twirly willow. Things need checking. They need watering with the hose. All these things out here need your attention. And I'll come round the garden with you and supervise what you're up to. Come away from that horrible computer thing and its terrible messages.

And he does. He spends an hour in the garden with me. I sit on the plank and observe.

I go back to the Beach House and flomp on the bed settee. Paul's left a few papers out here, some crumpled, some half written on. Some books are left open, scattered about. I curl up on the blanket and watch the magnolia tree and, beyond that, the trains running by the platform at Levenshulme.

Come Back

The day goes by quietly. Jeremy's got no one to talk to. There's no radio on, no telly. He works till late and I fall asleep on the settee downstairs. When he comes to fetch me, to take me to bed, he puts me on his shoulder, so I'm facing backwards. This is the way I like to be carried, so the boys have discovered. When my claws are too long, they can catch on the fabric of their jumpers and shirts and we sometimes get in a terrible tangle, and I have to do some shouting.

Tonight is peaceful, though, and I look backwards over Jeremy's shoulder as we go upstairs. This way I can see my reflection in all the mirrors in the downstairs hall, up the stairs, and on the top landing. My mouth is a tight, wonky line and I look worried.

"He'll come back tomorrow," Jeremy tells me as I jump from his shoulder onto their messy bed. "You'll see, Fester Cat."

I wake up and this side of the bed's too flat. Both sides are flat. Even Jeremy's not here. He's fallen asleep downstairs.

I remember what happened.

Paul doesn't come back all that day. He texts a message to say he'll be away for a few days.

GOOD-BYES

They can't split up. They can't say good-bye to each other.

Paul can't leave him. Hasn't he said good-bye enough in his life? That's what makes him sad. Deep down, I reckon. All those good-byes, all his life. Why would he want to make another one? How could he bring himself to leave?

I'm in the Beach House in the middle of the week, thinking it through. There's been no mammy cat ears. No bloomin' Bath Time song. No walking together down the plank to the little house. I came here alone and I'm thinking it through. Like, what if I have to sit here by myself forever now?

If they break up, what will happen to me?

Will Jeremy stay here alone? It would be a much quieter place. Paul talks all the time. He talks all day long to me, explaining everything and asking me questions. Jeremy gets on with things and it's like he himself is an animal. Like a super-intelligent dog, with hands. One who can work a computer and drive a car. He talks to me, but not in the same way. He can be quiet for very long stretches of time. He gives wonderful tickles and rubs my fur like no one can. His words are all on the inside, like most animals' are.

Where will Paul go? Will he move away to another place completely? Will he come back and visit sometimes? Will he stay away and try to forget us both? Will Jeremy be so angry that Paul's name will never be mentioned again?

I can't imagine any of this. I'm making myself smaller and smaller on the bed settee at the bottom of the garden. I'm curling into a tighter knot.

Then I'm listening to the squirrels running about on the roof of my house. They're going really fast and it's pretty obnoxious. They jump from the roof into the branches of the trees and then back again. They're doing it just to tease me, I reckon. I'll have a nap, and if they're still doing it in half an hour, I'll go and give them a chase.

Isn't it great? I feel like chasing things again. I feel like clouting those little beggars and banging their heads together. I feel like getting them in my claws and giving them what for.

Only a few weeks ago I was so hopeless. I hurt whenever I moved. But I've been busy, ever since my illness. Building all my strength back up.

I've been working hard to keep myself healthy. I wanted to be good and strong and alive for my boys.

I wonder if I catch some things — some mice and stuff — and take them in the house? Maybe that'll be an incentive to Paul to come back? Look! Look what I've been up to!

My Work

There are mice underneath our house.

Oh, I've been down in that cellar. I'm not supposed to, because of what happened before. When I used the whole of one room as a litter tray for a week. But I know that it's there. It's like a whole other house under there. There are just as many rooms, all of them dark, with a muddy floor. There are boxes — cardboard, mousey-smelling, slowly turning soft with damp and speckled mould. It's a heavenly place for a little cat. All those old books and papers. Folders and files, and bits of old furniture. Heaps of old videotapes that are blooming inside with mildewy flowers.

There are little holes in the skirting boards and between the bare boards of our downstairs rooms. I've taken careful note of them all. Sometimes there are knots in the wood that have been nibbled and chiseled away. It seems that it's only the very smallest mice that come up top to explore and hunt around. Baby mice, really, though this makes them even harder to catch, in my book.

Paul was horrified the first time he saw them. Wails and lamentations about living in a mucky house. Living in a slum. But it's an old house. It's below the water table, whatever that means. It means, I guess, that the cellar smells watery and brackish, which I love. And we're surrounded by wildlife, aren't we? There are animals everywhere. And all of it untamed and surging around us. Busy, hungry little bodies pushing their way towards where it's brightest, warmest.

Jeremy put down humane traps, but he put down poison as well. Paul found a mouse inside a dust bunny underneath the boiler in the kitchen during the winter. It was curled up and dried out and light as a feather. Its face was frozen in anguish. Jeremy said something about how it must have eaten the poison and crept to the warmest place in the room as it died. He said it so matter-of-factly Paul thought he was horrible and he almost cried. He felt sick to his stomach. But what are you supposed to do? Let all the animals come in to share your food and your life? You can't be that soft. That's ridiculous.

I patrol the perimeter of our lives. I've been in the ivy upon next door's shed. I've grabbed quite big mice by the scruff of their necks. I've cuffed them about their little skulls with my paws and knocked them senseless. They've fallen over, stunned, and lay quivering between my feet, then I hugged them to my chest, deciding what's to become of them. I'm a cat. I'm an expert in the field. I know what's what.

Since I've been back to full fitness I have given myself a new job. I am taking this mouse infestation business extremely seriously.

I station myself on the kitchen table. I sit like a vulture on the very corner, poised to spring.

What they're after, you see, is Fester's cat food. They come out of the holes in the wood and creep up to the feeding station. They clamber onto the smorgasbord. Seriously, I'm not making this up. It's a bloomin' outrage. You can hardly believe it. The brass neck of them. But I suppose they're desperate. What else is there to eat down in that cellar? Wormy things and those insects with the hard, nasty shells.

I sit there with my eyes narrowed. Watching as they sniff the air for Fester's special snacks and the glistening pouch food.

They're almost blind from living in the darkness down there. They're very dark, with pin-bright black eyes. Little mice, no bigger than one of my paws. Then —

POW!

I launch myself off the corner of the table. Head down, paws outstretched. Flinging myself straight at the smorgasbord.

There's a hell of a clatter. The dishes go everywhere. So does my glass of water. Food goes spattering through the air.

Sometimes they're too fast for me. They know I'm here. They're ready for me. They spring away on their skinny dark legs. But still they're hungry and out they come.

CLATTER! SMASH!

And maybe three times out of ten I get rewarded for my strenuous efforts. I get a mouse. A whole one. All to myself. Still living. Panting hard. Quivering with frantic life. (They're no fun dead, really, are they?)

I hold it in my mouth.

For best effect, hold it facing outwards. That way, when you take it to your human friends, they get the full effect. This little frightened face staring back at them out of their cat's mouth. Eyes popping out on stalks. Another good one is going up to your human with the tail hanging out of your mouth. Like a cigarette butt or a strand of

307

spaghetti. All casual. Do it quite nonchalantly. When I do this to Paul, when he's lying on the settee or reading, he howls. He goes crackers.

It's hilarious.

But when he's not here, is it even worth it?

What am I even bothering to catch mice for?

Oh yes. If I do this. If I keep working. If I keep doing my job. That'll bring him back. Yes. He'll come back if I keep doing this. That's it.

MISSING NO MORE

Of course he bloomin' comes back.

Jeremy goes to fetch him in the car.

Jasmine isn't best pleased, apparently. She lost patience with Paul after about a day of him staying with her. Maybe he talked too much. Maybe it was all about missing me, or missing Jeremy. Either way, after about a day of him staying at hers she was out of sympathy for him. When he told her that Jeremy had phoned and he was going back home, she looked annoyed. She was out when Jeremy came by to pick Paul up.

"Look who I've brought back, Fester!" Jeremy says, when they come through our front door later that afternoon.

I sit in the kitchen doorway. "Ungow," I tell them. Open a pouch for me. Unlock the back door and open it up. Let's look at the garden together. Put the kettle on. We're back to normal. Good.

Just as well.

My Nemesis Ralph

It's a long, lovely autumn.

The boys don't go on holiday because they both get too busy with work. They are learning to get along together again, after the ructions.

Jeremy is called to meetings by a committee. They discuss his work. He finds that his boss has raised some serious issues about him. The awful boss has got others on the committee believing in him. Jeremy's quietly getting worse, increasingly scared and struggling more.

My biggest problem is Ralph.

A new cat has moved in, three doors down. He's barely more than a kitten, but he's intent on making this street his own. A little tortoiseshell cat with a snarky attitude. Way too cocky for his own good. When he first pops over our fence I take careful note of him. I respond good-naturedly to his ragging and his messing about. I watch him from my veranda chair outside my Beach House.

He trots along the fences, bouncing after squirrels. He's got boundless energy, it seems.

As time goes on, though, he's a bit in your face.

It's all too much, having this little scrap of a thing dancing around you. He never says much. He doesn't have much conversation at all. He just dances around and tries to show off. Then he comes dashing up, trying to get me to play. He wants me to chase him.

As the months go by he gets bigger and stronger. He's too big to play games like this anymore. He isn't a kitten. He should know better than to dance around an elder like this.

But no one has taught Ralph how to behave. He's like a young punk, running wild on Chestnut Avenue.

Jeremy goes round Ralph's owners' house in the evening. He's friends with them and they play records, smoke cigarettes, and talk for hours. He comes back and tells Paul that Ralph is a complete sweetie at home. He's the meekest, friendliest little cat you could ever meet. They've got a baby, so of course they'd never have a wild, vicious cat any-where near. Ralph is okay. Jeremy says he lies in a woolly cot affair that straps to their kitchen radiator. He's looking like butter wouldn't melt when he's at home.

I try telling them. He's a crazed jungle beast out there in the garden backs.

There are a number of fights.

He starts them.

I can't help but be drawn in. I'm just defending myself. My patch.

Paul hears us first every time and he goes dashing out. He flings a cup of cold tea or a bucket of water, whatever comes to hand first. He says that when we're fighting we look just like cartoon cats. Like a large whirling cloud of dust, with shreds of fur and claws flying out all over the place. And the noise is earsplitting! Terrifying!

Myself, I hate fighting. But sometimes it just has to be done.

I get a big scratch on the perfect white felt of my nose. Paul is appalled by this.

"His fur is so perfect. It's like the velvet inside an antique jewellery box. Or inside a case for a violin. And now there's a dirty great scratch across his nose."

During one fight Ralph gives me a nasty bite on the scruff of the neck. Nobody notices it afterwards. But in the days that follow I can feel it turning horrible. It swells inside me like a boil. My skin goes stretched and stiff feeling. Ralph's horrible saliva curdles in the wound.

Then, one morning when Paul's on his way to work, I make him sit for a few moments with me on his knee. Just as he's stroking my shoulders the wound bursts and all this hideous pus comes out. Yellow as custard and all Ralph's fault. Ralph and his filthy, dirty mouth.

So that's me back at the hairdresser's. More antibiotics. More pills to take in the morning with my chicken liver pâté. At the supermarket Paul has found some cat snacks that are like long straws made out of meat, with pâté inside. He breaks them into little pieces and pops the pills inside for me. We call them cat cigars, and on the whole I'd say they were most satisfying.

While my neck wound is healing I have to wear a bandage round my neck. It's tied securely and goes under one leg. It's all a bit of a bind. I'm sure I look silly, even if Paul says I actually look like a tough bandit, or a pirate. But without the bandage, I'm sure the boys are right, I'd scratch the hell out of the healing wound on my neck. I'd make it worse than ever. And so I have to live with this horrible bloomin' bandage. Jeremy takes a photo of me and catches me mid-ablutions. I look like I'm sticking my tongue out at the camera.

Ralph has a vendetta. I find that I can't stand at the front of our house without him catching my scent and bounding up. Or he lies in wait with his hackles raised. He just wants to fight me. He's had a taste of my blood and that's it. He's after me.

The boys decide that I can't go out front alone. They can't trust Ralph. And they can't trust me not to fight him back.

Even in the back garden it's not safe to leave me alone. Ralph comes scaling over the tall fence, watching for when I'm on my own. Paul overreacts a bit, I must admit. He says that either he or Jeremy has to be out there with me, every time I go outside. I think that's overdoing it, but I don't say anything. I'm very glad of the company.

And what a wonderful slow autumn it is for sitting outside. The days hold their warmth until it's completely dark. Everything gets covered in wonderful red and yellow leaves. We lie on the bed settee with throws over us, reading for hours.

Trying to forget the world beyond our house and our back garden.

PETER

It's Book Club one night and Paul's at Karen's house down the street. For once there's a pretty heated debate going on among the members. A debate that's actually about the month's chosen book! Then, all of a sudden, Jeremy comes banging on the door. He looks very upset.

He says to Paul, "Can you come home? My father's just died."

Suddenly everyone's on their feet. The boys are hugging, and then Paul and Jeremy are hurrying back to our house.

I stand on the kitchen table to see and hear better as Jeremy explains to Paul.

This is Peter, isn't it? I'm thinking as I listen. The old gent whose lap I sit on at Christmas.

Jeremy tells his story quickly. His mother just phoned him. Peter died suddenly this afternoon. He was midsentence and he fell into his wife's arms and was gone in an instant.

We're shocked, listening to this, me and Paul.

He was here, just a few weeks ago. Peter and Rita were both here, in the days before Christmas. They stayed in a hotel and they all had dinner out together in a fancy place. Then another night, Paul cooked a big roast here and they sat in the dining room, with the tree half decorated and Fester Cat sitting at his own chair. "Come on, old fella," Peter said. "Come and sit in your usual spot."

Everyone had a glass of bubbly and they played their silly board games again, laughing a lot. And I watched them all and joined in when I could.

And now Peter has gone. He was a splendid age for a human being, I hear. And up till the end he was out in his garden. He was doing things like scaling walls to cut down hedges. He was climbing ladders when he knew he oughtn't. He had so much energy he was helping neighbours out with looking after their gardens.

There's a stunned silence in our house as the boys get ready to travel to Scotland.

It will be strange for them, going there and seeing all the space where he isn't anymore. Expecting him to walk into the room at any moment. I already know what all of that's like. I've got a lot of friends and faces I knew that I don't ever see anymore.

The boys go away and I watch from the top window. They're quiet and thoughtful when they go. They fuss over me and they don't even know when they'll be back. They tell me that Karen and Mark will come by to feed me, and that both neighbours know how to give me my special tablets properly. So that will be okay. We're calling my pink tablets "biscuits" these days. I will do my best to take them, and not cause a fuss. I won't have any of my awkward days, not with the neighbours.

So I have wintry days at home in the house by myself. To snooze and think. Radio 3 plays all day long and the air feels syrupy with all that classical music. Snow blows through town and I remember the wintry days outside, when Jeremy coaxed me to walk on the fresh-fallen snow. When I watched him build a panda made out of snow, and darted back indoors as soon as I could. I love to watch the flakes falling, though, as I perch on the back of the settee.

Days and days pass. In Scotland there's a hundred and one things for them to do. All the human rituals to do with death. The

318

vicar comes and wants to read a sermon all about fire and brimstone, heaven and hell. Jeremy gets a bit miffed and tells him Peter wasn't big on that kind of religion. But the vicar still wants to read these particular verses, and so Jeremy sacks him, and they get a nice lady to do it instead.

Al Bowlly songs will play. Music coming out of a different era. The lady vicar reads a thing out about setting off in a ship. And how everyone should be excited for the one departing. He's setting off somewhere new.

WOOZY

Sometime after they come back, I catch a chill. I start sneezing. At first it sounds cute, but then the sneezes become more violent. Jeremy's sitting up in bed watching me. He's lying in. I'm stretching and walking across the duvet towards him for a cuddle. Paul's already out somewhere, having a coffee meeting with a friend in Heaton Chapel.

Jeremy's watching me when I give one of my loudest sneezes. I lose my balance and fall onto the duvet. I jump up again, shaking my head. But I'm woozy. Jeremy says I look disoriented, when he phones Paul to tell him.

"I think he might have had a stroke."

All at once Paul feels weirdly guilty for being out this morning. He's laughing in a café instead of at his desk, working and having coffee with me. Because he has broken our morning routine, things have gone wrong. That's what he thinks. Because I looked for him and he wasn't there and I headed back to bed with Jeremy, I have become ill. I have had a funny turn.

Paul races back. They both watch me carefully.

I'm not off my food. They think my eyes might be doing something strange. Scanning back and forth, and then settling down. I look at some rooms as if I'm not sure where I am.

They get me to the hairdresser's. But there they get told that I've just got an infection. Something to do with my ear that makes me lose balance.

I keep sneezing and sneezing all that day.

"Maybe I should dust more," Paul says. "Or maybe I shouldn't dust so much? Maybe it's dust flying about that makes him sneeze?"

"It isn't that," says Jeremy. "It isn't dust. You heard. It's germs he's got. Just a little flu, like people get at this time of year."

I lie on my blue blanket and feel quite sorry for myself for several days. I didn't like that woozy, dizzy feeling much, I can tell you. It made me feel helpless. Like I was falling out of the sky. Like I was heading for a fall.

But when my germs clear up and I stop sneezing, I decide a little dizziness isn't going to hold me back. I'm up on the kitchen table dive-bombing again and pouncing on mice. I'm out in the garden again, doing a poo amongst the bushes and racing away from it as fast as I can.

I'm determined to get back to normal and ignore that foggy dizziness that sometimes creeps into the corner of my vision. The woozy feeling. That's got nothing to do with me.

I focus on my daily tasks. Getting Paul up and about in the morning, walking him through his routines. Taking my biscuit and sitting beside him at his desk. The two of us posing for our regular pictures together and posting them so people can see us on his blog. Working hard and getting our pages done. Writing our books.

One day I bring him a little bird. I've popped into the back garden while he's working and, as I mooched in the undergrowth, found this tiny blue bird sitting on a branch. It didn't seem to have much idea about anything, so I leaned forward and scooped it up in my mouth. Then I trotted indoors and up the stairs to show Paul and then Jeremy.

They were both horrified. Really, I think their reactions were way over-the-top. Apparently at first it looked comical. I opened my mouth and there was a baby bird's face looking out. Its tiny beak was open in outrage. It didn't look frightened at all. Just furious to find itself half swallowed on its first day out, flying around.

Jeremy managed to hook his finger around it to get it out of my mouth. It was a tiny thing and for a second I felt ashamed. Catching such a fun-sized morsel and feeling so proud. It was a damp blue tit, dwarfed in Jeremy's palm, sticky with cat spit.

He took it outside once it was dry and calmed it down a little, and set it upon the wall.

"Someone else will come along and eat it," I pointed out. "Someone crueler and more hungry than me."

But they watched it until it was okay again and ready to fly away.

Ah well. It's not like I was actually intending to eat it. The main thing was for me to prove that I've still got *it*.

It: that indefinable catty blend of the killer instinct, bravado, and playful wit.

When the garden warms up and the frogs start lazing about in the pond, I decide to surprise everyone and try the same thing with one of our amphibious friends. He's sunbathing at the side of the pond and I pretend I'm just having a drink. Then as

I'm sauntering casually by I suddenly whip round and clasp my bloomin' jaws around him. *Snap.*

It is the most disgusting thing I have ever felt or tasted inside my mouth.

He squirms against my gums and I drop him at once.

Then I go tearing back up the garden path, across the patio, and up the steps at full pelt. I race inside the house. Up the stairs, down the hall, and I take a flying leap at Paul's desk, where he's working, wholly absorbed in what he's writing. With a huge clatter of legs and claws I skid across his desk and end up crashing into the window.

He looks a bit surprised. When I turn to him with horrible greenish stuff drooling out of my mouth, he looks even more surprised.

I tell him: "I've been trying to eat a frog."

But I don't think I'll be trying that again. Paul helps me mop myself up. And then I head for the bedroom and the glass of water on his table. I shove in my whole head, drinking as deep as I can.

FULL-TIME

Paul's having coffee in town. He's leaving his job at the university for the last time.

He's been working up to this for ages. Now he's writing in his journal about being free to write what he wants, and to think about what he wants. This morning he's taken several large bags of novel manuscripts back to the office. All marked, with reports attached. I've sat with him for days and days while he did them. When he put in his notice he was given a mammoth amount of work to do. It was just spite, he knew it. How many millions of words could he read and mark in a few weeks?

But now it's done.

Now he's sitting here, he's thinking how silly it is anyway. Giving a mark to a novel. Giving it a percentage. Sitting in schoolrooms and talking about these things. Novels belong in the wild, he thinks. Or if not the wild, in back gardens and bedrooms.

He's drinking a soupy latte and thinking about being free to write full-time. Something he's never done before.

He rings ahead and tells Jeremy he's on his way home.

And when he gets off the train at Levenshulme, something funny happens. It's a sunny morning and he's swinging his empty book bag as he walks down Beech Tree Road.

There's a yowl from a tabby being chased out of a garden into the street. Paul pauses as it races past, and then he sees who it's being chased by.

"Bessy!"

And there she is. Looking a bit more beat-up than before. With a nick out of one of her ears. And looking completely startled when Paul cries out her name.

"Come home, Bessy," he says. "Come and see the others!"

And she follows him, all down the street, round the corner onto Sycamore Avenue, and beyond into Chestnut Avenue. Every few yards she can't help herself flomping with delight onto the tarmac. She blows all her cool but she doesn't care. He stops to tickle her for a few moments and tells her how everyone will be so pleased to see her again. "Where've you been, girl? Living rough again?"

The pair of them arrive back at our house like a triumphant parade. Paul's jacked in his job in that department where he wasn't happy! Bessy's back home at last!

They dash through the house into the back garden, where I'm sitting on my plank and Jeremy's moving a tree.

"Bessy!" I gasp.

"Hiya," she says, as if she's never been away.

WHAT'S GOING ON

But over the next day or two I see that Bessy's exhausted. She's seeming much older than she was. Living rough takes it out of you.

"There are fewer empty lots and derelict houses now," she tells me. "They've all been done up as luxury apartments and all that rubbish. *Ffffft.* There used to be rich pickings round here. Now it's all down by the railway embankment. That's where everyone's living, all a bit crushed together. It's a fiercer place."

I tell her that's what the whole world's gone like. It's a meaner, poorer place these days. That Albert fella was right, in a way. The world was having a disaster and even Bessy and her rough friends were feeling it, living by the railway lines.

"So, what's been happening here?" she asks, with a snicker. Like she thinks nothing very important or dramatic ever happens round our house. She thinks all we do all day is lie about in the sun. "I've kept my eye on you lot," she says. "I've seen you in your chichi little shed. I've seen your fancy barbecues with the neighbours."

"You were watching?"

"From up on the railway lines. Yeah. But I never really felt like coming back. This is just a fleeting visit, you know."

"Is it?" I ask her. "I don't think the boys realise that."

"That daft pair." She tosses her head. "Are they married yet?"

"Not yet. They wanted to have a do, with a party in the garden and everything. They were really thinking about it. But then Jeremy's dad died. Everything's been put on hold. They don't want a wedding if he can't be there. Not yet."

"Putting things off is bad," Bessy says. "Next thing you know, the time is gone."

I think she might have been getting a bit philosophical as she sheltered from the cold and wet by the railway lines. She's sounding a lot like Smokey in her old age.

"And now there's all these ructions with Paul's family," I tell her. "They've started leaving horrible messages on the phone and on Facebook. I don't quite understand what's going on there. And also, Jeremy was made to leave his job . . ."

"He's left his job!" gasps Bessy.

"He was made so unhappy he had to leave it," I correct myself. "It was horrible. And now Paul has gone and left his too . . ."

"What?!" Bessy squawks.

"Paul had to leave. He has to write. He's had twenty years teaching and it was doing his head in. That university was a terrible place to be."

"But they'll have no money! They'll have nothing to live on!" Bessy is flabbergasted. "What do they think they're doing?"

I don't have an answer to that. I know I'm just glad the two of them will be at home more in future. Jeremy hasn't got that awful stress anymore. Neither has Paul. I was worried about them.

Bessy, though, is scandalised. "But no money, Fester Cat. Maybe they'll decide that they can't afford that expensive cat food you like to eat? What if they decide that you're a luxury they just can't afford?"

"Never!" I gasp. "They'd never do that!"

"They might," she says. "How much do those daily tablets of yours cost, eh?"

Now I remember why Bessy used to annoy me so much of the bloomin' time. She sets out to wind me up. She's deliberately unsettling me. I need to rise above it.

She sees that I won't argue with her, and she goes to lie down in the long grass under the magnolia.

"I suppose this garden is pretty okay now," she says. "It's all right."

But I don't need to hear Bessy's approval about anything. I know it's all perfect out here. Our lives together are perfect. And maybe there won't be as much money. And maybe Paul's family is being a bit strange and relations are very strained. But we're together here and that's what counts.

Bessy stays for dinner on the patio.

"It's odd, having Bessy back," Paul says.

Jeremy's frowning at her. "My God! Have you ever noticed?"

"Hmm?"

"Bessy's got two huge hairy bollocks!"

She carries on eating from her old bowl and pretends she hasn't heard a word of this.

She sticks around for a day or so, catching up with every scrap of news. She cleans herself and watches some telly with us, and decides all over again that a simple homebody life isn't for her.

"I'll be off now, then," she tells us, and slinks, for the very last time, into the grass.

ENJOY

Thoroughly enjoying yourself and being happy.

That's what it's all about.

These days I love doing things like drinking from the pond. Paul watches carefully when I do, in case I shake my head and lose my balance. He has a fear of me falling in the deep water, but I never do.

I love going back to my plank down the middle of the garden. From there I can see everything going on.

I love to spend whole days on the veranda of the sleepy Beach House. This summer is, I believe, the best one ever, because Paul puts a sun lounger on the grass and covers it with stripy cushions. I lie on them, or on him, when he reads. It's all perfect. He pulls a shade over when the sun is highest.

The most important thing is that those of us in our family, living here, are happy being in the same place.

Paul does Sunday lunch for a bunch of people. They sit outside with cold green soup and roasted chicken, then baked plums with toasted almonds. Usually I'd be sniffing round and joining them. But it's the friends who aren't really my favourites. Albert and Jasmine and others. Why does he keep trying to hold on to friends I don't really care for? Can't he see through them like I can? I make my feelings plain by going to hide under the settee in the Beach House.

Another Sunday there's a raucous barbecue with a real party atmosphere, and I decide to grace this one with my presence. Nibbling a tender piece of chicken on the back steps and greeting the friends that I approve of. I like this lot. "Ungow."

Sometime that summer Paul's family declares they're moving to Australia. They do it on Facebook, announcing to the world that there's nothing for them here in England. No grandchildren, no children with money to give them. They don't like spending time with Paul and Jeremy. Jeremy's a jobless fool who talks to a panda. Paul's mam phones up to scream at him. His sister sends taunting text messages. It's all very confusing. There are some kinds of human behaviour that cats don't understand. "But we took them on holiday!" Jeremy gasps. "We took them on a Mediterranean cruise and blew all our money!"

I try to tell them: It doesn't matter. Let them carry on how they want. Don't get drawn into arguments. Some people will spend all their lives causing arguments. It's because they enjoy it.

In the end, they just bloomin' enjoy it.

They like causing misery because they don't believe in happiness.

Other people — people like us — we prefer a bit of peace.

Put all of that aside. Look at us! We're together! That's all we need. Our family together. Let's have our very best summer's end, and autumn and Christmas ever.

We've spent all this time together. We have this history. More than six years of it.

At Christmas I go crazy, ripping into gift wrap and playing with all my toys. I chase the turkey heart again and sit at the posh table with the boys for our dinner. By the evening I am worn out and they take a picture of me cuddling this toy mouse in his Santa hat.

The boys are pleased I have such a great Christmas because halfway through December I was ill again for a few days with another infection. I lost my voice, which was strange indeed. It reminded me of when I used to wear bells on my collar and I'd jingle for attention. When my voice comes back it's very high for a few days. I go round sounding quite amazed. For a part of December I can't even say "Ungow" properly. "Oh wow? Oh wow?"

But the infection fades. I rally in time for the festivities. I try hard to put the weight back on. But it's a very cold, cold time of year. I'm happiest on the orange settee watching films with my boys. The happiest night all Christmas is spent in front of *Flash Gordon*. Their friends Nick and Jon from London visit for haggis, neeps and tatties while they all watch *Mame*. They return from fireworks at the neighbours' house to watch *The Rocky Horror Picture Show* in the middle of the night. On New Year's Day Paul lies down between bouts of cooking and I lie with him to watch *The Sound of Music* and *The Wizard of Oz*.

Of course, we've seen all these films together before. But that's the whole point of it. These are our favourites. We know just how to enjoy ourselves.

I lie on his chest and push my face into his. Touch his nose with mine. *BOOP.*

THE NEW YEAR

We love our early mornings.

Well, Paul and I do. I wake him when first light is showing. In these first days of January we don't hurry to have breakfast. We lie still. Paul does some early-morning reading with me lying there on his chest. We're close by the window and we're watching the snow. It's all blue outside. We're in our bedroom full of books and the bedside lamp is pink. I'm stretched out on my blue blanky. And it's so, so quiet.

And as the new year comes to life we love starting to do our favourite days again. We're working and looking at the street outside. Paul's drinking coffee Jeremy has brought for him and Paul's scrolling through his pages on the screen. I sit by his laptop and watch from the window. I'm seeing all the local cats running about, and I'm watching Lexy the daft terrier from next door sniffing at bushes and cars. And I'm hearing tales about Fang, the new, growing kitten down the street at Karen and Mark's.

And it strikes me that all the animals round here have changed about.

Wood pigeons. I can hear them cooing from the back garden. They're always there, just the same.

Paul spends his days thinking all about work. One project has bitten the dust unexpectedly. He's been dumped unceremoniously by his main publisher. They wanted him to become more ordinary. More like everyone else. And he wouldn't even know where to start.

Now he's waiting to hear about a book he wrote last year, and whether people want to buy it. Now he's struggling with beginning a new book about something else.

And this is the way we go on.

Then — one day — I suddenly feel a lot older. I feel distracted. Just a little confused.

I call for Paul. I'm standing at the doorway of the bathroom.

"Paaa-aaaauuuu-aaauulll?"

But I know where he is. Of course I do. He's just across the landing. In his tiny study. I can see him in his new cardy. I know he's sitting there. Why am I calling out like I can't find him? My voice sounds desperate and lost-sounding. It sounds alarming even to me. Paul comes hurrying over. "What is it, Fester Cat?" He picks me up. "Come and sit with me. Come and sit on this chair beside my desk . . ."

Later, there I am drinking water on the bedside table in the middle of the night. Always thirsty these days. Then I stop. What am I supposed to be doing? I feel puzzled. I feel like I have an appointment somewhere and I've only just remembered.

Doddery? Is that how I am? Paul uses the word.

Sometime around now I start forgetting about my litter tray. I take to pooing and weeing on the bathroom rugs. The white tufted one from Habitat feels so tempting under my feet, you see. Like superior-quality grass. The boys don't mind chucking all the rugs in the wash every day. What does it matter?

But it's strange for me. Forgetting how to do things. Not knowing what the right way is.

Now there's a long weekend coming up and Jeremy's birthday.

It even feels like the wintry weather might be coming to an end.

All we want is a calm time together. With some delicious food, maybe.

All my boys together for a long weekend.

But now I've got a headache coming. I can feel a thirst and it's getting bigger. I feel an endless thirstiness. And there's a dizziness and a nagging thought — where am I supposed to be?

This time last year it was so much warmer. There was pink and white blossom hanging from the trees and swaying in the gentle wind. There were deck chairs and drinking out of the green pond, which wasn't coated in ice. There was sitting in Fester's chair on the veranda on striped cushions. All day long.

It's outside, isn't it? That's where we should be, isn't it?

But the bloomin' weather changes again. It snows all over the country and some places have drifts. Here in Manchester, it only tries to snow. We only get a little. But still it freezes. The weather feels cruel. Then it rains hard, and it's freezing cold and the drafts come sweeping indoors and up through the bare boards.

On the Monday before Easter, me and Paul are looking out of the sitting room window. All of a sudden we see that the snow has stopped.

Now the sun comes out and it's gently mopping up the damp. It's even getting warm.

We stretch in the new heat as it blares through the window.

Paul asks, "Shall we go out into the garden, little cat?"

"Ungow?" I ask. "Shall we? Is it time?"

It's time to open the stiff back door. Time to pad across the concrete. Time to totter down the gravel path. And to balance along the plank towards the Beach House.

"Shall we open up the little house and let the air back in? Breathe in the trapped scents of cat hair and old books and last year's grass and leaves?

"Shall we sit in the first of the sun?"

Maybe we can urge the spring to come along faster. We could cheer it on. We can watch the clouds spreading over and the sun coming through the branches. We can watch the squirrels dashing madly, building stuff, stealing things . . . doing all their usual business.

"Shall we go and sit at the bottom of the garden, Fester? At last?"

"Ungow!"

"Let's go!"

SOMETHING I WANT TO TELL YOU BOTH

I want to sit with you in the Beach House now and tell you this. It's important.

I want you to remember all of this.

All these days.

Because I'll only be *part* of the story.

I know your human lives are generally longer than cats'. And you had all that life before we met and before I was born. You'll have lots more life afterwards, I hope. And maybe you'll have more cats! There may be other cats in your future! I don't know. I can't imagine what they might be like.

But I want you to remember this.

These long and happy days together.

And don't forget me?

Keep me separate and special.

I know the human mind is bigger, with much more room. The cat mind seems smaller.

But I know I would never forget any of this.

Thank you for keeping me going. I've had extra years because of you both. They've been the best.

And, in the future, if you ever happen to look up and see me standing there — up a tree, through the leaves, on the fence, or between the banisters of your staircase on my way to bed — I can't promise to be there.

I'm sorry. But I can't.

I can't come running to you anymore.

But I did, didn't I?

All those times.

I came running to you like no one else ever did.

And it's not everyone who can know what

that's like. To have Fester Cat running to them. As fast as he bloomin' well can. Excited forever. Ungow!

Running to be with you.

AFTERWORD BY PAUL

Sometimes you have to trust other people with your story. And to get the end of your story right.

He placed his life in our hands the day that he decided to adopt us. He took a few days and a few visits and a few free feeds to decide. But when Fester decided that our house was where he wanted to live for the rest of his life, it was wholehearted and ir-reversible. He always had a fierce energy and spirit. He always knew his own mind.

And so in he moved and he trusted us with the rest of his story.

We've figured out that he was eighteen when he died and he was twelve when he moved in. It was the final third of his life that he was trusting us with.

He had been a stray. He was in a bad way. His fur was tattered and there were bare patches. Every bit of his skin was scabbed from fleabites. He was incredibly thin and mangy. He was silent, just about. Watchful, weighing up. He was starved. He only had one and a half teeth and his gums were mangled and swollen and obviously sore.

When he moved in we got him fixed up. He had every kind of makeover and medical thing you could think of. We had his teeth fixed. We had him chipped. When we knew he belonged to no one else and this little cat was completely ours, we made the deal permanent. And we knew that this would mean one day facing the end of his life. That's how it goes.

And so that's what we've just been facing.

It's just been the end of his story. This Easter weekend. It's only Easter Monday now. We're still in shock, I think. We've spent the weekend crying and talking and looking at pictures and looking at drawings and finding even more photos. And then

346

sitting in the garden in the sun.

This morning I've been writing about his final week with us. The words have just been pouring out of me. It was one thousand, two thousand, three thousand, four . . . my fingers flickering over the keys of my laptop. Like I thought if I kept on typing and never stopped, I wouldn't look up at the rest of my desk and see that he wasn't sitting there. Usually he'd be perched very tidily, looking out of the window until the drama of Chestnut Avenue out there faded down and he'd turn to me and come for a kiss, a nudge, or to interpose himself between me and my keyboard. He knew when roughly twelve hundred words had gone by. He knew it was time to save me from my obsessive writing. He knew he could get me to stop, to make a trip downstairs for a cup of tea and to feed him a snack.

But, this sunny Easter Monday I was alone and kept typing. Four thousand, five thousand, six thousand words.

Every thousand I would save the file and e-mail it to myself. I don't want to chance things and lose any of it. I can't lose any of it, I'm telling myself. I have to save everything. Just like I'm trying to remember everything before it starts to fade.

Most writers I know have a touch of the

obsessive-compulsive disorders. It comes with the gig, I reckon. And the obsessive recording of details that other people might find trivial is just the kind of thing that I need to keep hold of. Those details are the fabric of life.

Folk with OCD like I've got believe that if you don't hang on to the little memories and all their tiny details, something awful will happen to you and those you love.

But, here and now, something awful has already happened. We have lost our Fester Cat. And so I'm trying to remember my way back. I'm trying to bring him back through sheer willpower and concentration. I believe I can will him back to life on the page.

That's how writers with OCD and all dafties think. I realise that.

And I write the end of his story, the final week our family had together, because if I don't do it now, it will start to slip away. Little drib by drab, piece by piece. The little patterns in the fabric that make it so rich — they'll be the first to go.

I woke up this morning with no one to shout at me, telling me to get up and feed him. No one crying out for that instant attention and love.

Jeremy sleeps. In crises and depression he sleeps straight through. Today he slept till twelve, until his friends came to take him out for lunch, a belated birthday treat.

I stayed here. I stayed here to blaze my way back into last week. I want to recall everything. Everything that went on last Monday, especially. When Fester was first ill and when, sometime during that day, he somehow had a stroke. My diary records he seemed older and unsure that day, even amongst the flomping and nudges and the cuddling up outside while I worked. Already bits of last Monday are slipping away from me. But that's the human way. We forget things in order to make room for the new weeks and new years we move into. We can't remember everything, we can't hold on to everything. We must make room.

But our house is cluttered with all the stuff we've held on to. My books are filled with details I've tried to rescue from oblivion.

I need to write the end of Fester's story, now and today, before it turns into something too smooth and finished. Something that misses the terror and exhaustion that the week put us through. And the fun and the love as well. And the little moments of triumph amongst the longer, surer arc that led to the finish.

Only when I've got all of that down, I thought, can I return to the beginning and tell the story of his life with us.

These are familiar, consoling sensations to me. The excitement of writing pages and pages and thousands and thousands of words. And the anticipation of returning to the start of the story and getting ready to tell all. And having a lead character I adore.

I'm making myself feel better not through immersing myself in work and busyness. But by going back to Fester. Finding my way back to him.

I know where he is. I know how he sounds.

He's in the garden, waiting.

All last week I hardly read anything at all.

I was struggling to reread my ancient, crappy paperback of Michael Ende's masterful kids' fantasy novel, *The Neverending Story*. My copy has the tiniest print imaginable and some previous owner has scrawled daft pencil marks on many of the pages. Even now I'm only about a hundred pages back into that wonderful epic.

Something I've been reminded of, though.

There's a motif running through the book. It usually goes something like this:

"And so they turned off at the next path, and although they left this particular story, they carried on having adventures of their own. And maybe one day we'll get to hear all about them."

I'm paraphrasing, but that's the idea.

For me this has to be one of the most important sentiments in the book. In fiction generally. Any kind of fiction.

The promise that these people — these friends, family, colleagues, lovers, characters. Everyone who ever leaves you and your story; who chooses to or finds they have to leave your side — they will carry on having their own adventures elsewhere. And somewhere, somehow, that is what's happening.

And one day you will find them again and catch up and hear what's been going on.

It's one of the oldest ideas in the book. In any book.

Rereading *The Neverending Story* last week, I had Fester purring on my knee. He dozed and gradually lost control of all of his body. He became lighter and lighter in my arms. It was like he was becoming even less than skin and bone. He was turning into paper.

In *The Neverending Story* every character peels off and away.

Everyone goes into their own imaginary spin-off tale.

This is important to me.

As I get older I realise that everyone is in a spin-off. There is no main story. No central character. We're all spinning off into our own adventures and only we are responsible for where that takes us.

Sometimes you've got to let your friends and companions split off along their own way. You have to wave them off.

Eventually you might hear from them again. There might even be a reunion tale.

That's how I was thinking, last week, a little sentimentally, perhaps. Life works like the very best stories. I've always thought that was true.

And when a turning point in a story is reached and a parting must happen, it makes you look back and take stock of the period you all spent together. You see that part of that story as a finished thing in itself. And to me it's important that you tell that well, succinctly and with spirit.

Here's me trying to do that.

In the six, almost seven years that Fester was with us, I believe he taught us to be a family. In many ways the odds have been against us. There have been some awful things going on in that time, outside and inside our house. From the grandness of a global economic collapse, to the dreadfulness of lost parents and bitter family feuds, down to the microcosmic detail of the day-to-day problems of careers gone crazy. We've had it all going on round here.

But through all of the past six or seven years Fester has been our constant. He taught us how to live in one house together, after Jeremy and I had been together for ten years and lived in different cities and tried to do the long-distance relationship thing that so many people have to do because of work and circumstances. This house was the first time we ever settled properly in one place and spread out, with all our stuff under one roof, pooling all our dreams and building a home and a garden and a future together. It was the place we found in our midthirties. In South Manchester, alongside the railway lines.

And only then did Fester come marching out of the undergrowth and up our back garden, demanding to be let into our house and our lives. This cat who must have been a kitten back in the midnineties, back in the days when Jeremy and I first met, up in Edinburgh. They were heady days, a long time ago, when Fester was only a kitten and Jeremy and I decided that we had found each other at last and this was it.

Fester was waiting for us all that time. Until he was twelve. Until we were in our house on Chestnut Avenue.

He wanted us to be there, sitting nicely, where he could see the pair of us together.

He was content and could sleep when we were settled in the living room, or on the patio, or were falling asleep in our bed. He'd stand on the duvet, watching till he knew we were dropping off and sometimes he'd go and keep watch on the landing. "Looking out for monsters," Jeremy always called it.

This is what Fester did. He was all about the value of sitting down nicely. Like a Zen master, he knew it was all about the sitting and breathing and relaxing. You could tell his whole life's narrative in the form of a list of favourite perches he found and why each one was essential. He loved long spells in safe havens and special spots. Curling up and being content with doing nothing but just sitting and singing and breathing and working towards the most contented of deep-felt sighs. This was something he taught me to share. Work towards that biggest sigh and that's you in the moment like never before.

That was the kind of wisdom he brought here — up our back garden, up the back stairs, into our kitchen. We just thought he was starving and glad to have some bits of bacon to chew on with his painful one and a half teeth. But no, he had a whole lot of stuff to unpack and impart to us. And it took the full six and a half years between 2006 and now.

He was teaching us and we were learning to be older, happier, and more still. He came from outside in order to teach us how to live in a house.

Fester's accomplishment for me was that he made being happy seem easy. Not just for me. For everyone he met. They all felt it. He made it seem easy to be content.

More than that.

He was all about showing us that it's actually easy to live happily. Easier than staying miserable any day.

It's something I hope I never forget.

Which is why I have to write it down.

And remember that there's a garden out there, and a Beach House. And there's always going to be a little cat out there, ready to remind you to be happy, and to remind you of everything you almost nearly forget.

Ungow, Fester.

Xx
Paul
Levenshulme, Manchester
Spring 2013

ABOUT THE AUTHOR

Paul Magrs is the author of many books, written for all ages and in many different genres, including the Adventures of Brenda and Effie and numerous *Doctor Who* novels, radio plays, and short stories. However, this is his first foray into memoir. He taught novel writing in the MA program in Creative Writing at UEA, and then at Manchester Metropolitan. Paul lives in Manchester, England, with his partner, Jeremy, and is now a full-time writer.

The employees of Thorndike Press hope you have enjoyed this Large Print book. All our Thorndike, Wheeler, and Kennebec Large Print titles are designed for easy reading, and all our books are made to last. Other Thorndike Press Large Print books are available at your library, through selected bookstores, or directly from us.

For information about titles, please call:
  (800) 223-1244

or visit our Web site at:
  http://gale.cengage.com/thorndike

To share your comments, please write:
  Publisher
  Thorndike Press
  10 Water St., Suite 310
  Waterville, ME 04901

.

ML   5-15